STOIC
LOGIC

BENSON MATES

STOIC LOGIC

UNIVERSITY OF CALIFORNIA PRESS

BERKELEY AND LOS ANGELES

1961

University of California Press
Berkeley and Los Angeles, California

Cambridge University Press
London, England

Originally published in 1953 as Volume 26
of the University of California
Publications in Philosophy

Second printing, 1961
(First Paper-bound Trade Edition)

Printed in the United States of America

PREFACE

During the eight years since this book was first published a number of scholars have made important contributions to the subject. The following items are especially worthy of note:

Sextus Empiricus. *Opera.* Ed. H. Mutschmann, with emendations, additions and corrections by Dr. Jürgen Mau; Leipzig, Teubner, 1954 (vol. 3), and 1958 (vol. 1). This new edition of the Teubner *Sextus* is a vast improvement; it provides a thoroughly reliable text, which, together with the complete indices contributed by Dr. Karl Janáček to volume 3, will greatly facilitate all future scholarship on the subject.

Galen. *Einführung in die Logik.* Critical and exegetical commentary, with German translation, by Dr. Jürgen Mau. Deutsche Akademie der Wissenschaften zu Berlin, Berlin, Akademie-Verlag, 1960. Dr. Mau here presents a definitive study of Galen's *Introduction to Logic.*

Becker, Oskar. *Ueber die vier Themata der stoischen Logik,* in *Zwei Untersuchungen zur Antiken Logik,* Wiesbaden, Otto Harrassowitz, 1957. Professor Becker has been remarkably successful in his attempt to make a plausible reconstruction of the lost 'Fourth Thema' of the Stoics (cf. pp. 77–82, below). His essay throws light upon the other Themata as well.

Bocheński, I. M. *Formale Logik.* Freiburg and Munich, Karl Alber, 1956. This source book is a major contribution to the history of logic, and especially to the history of ancient logic. It is indispensable for the reader who wishes to understand Stoic logic in relation to the developments which preceded it and to those which followed it.

Prior, A. N. "Diodoran Modalities," *Philosophical Quarterly,* vol. 5 (1955), pp. 205–213. In this interesting study of the so-called "Master" argument (cf. pp. 38–39, below), Professor Prior investigates the logical properties of Diodorean implication. Cf. also the same author's *Time and Modality,* Oxford, Clarendon Press, 1957, *passim,* and "Diodorus and Modal Logic," *Philosophical Quarterly,* vol. 8 (1958), pp. 226–230.

Casari, Ettore. "Sulla disgiunzione nella logica megarico-stoica," *Proceedings of the 8th International Congress for the History of Science*, pp. 1217–1224. Dr. Casari shows the importance of non-truth–functional connectives in Stoic logic.

It is perhaps not superfluous to mention that if I were writing this book over again, the principal change I would make would be to tone down or omit altogether my criticism of other authors. This criticism now affects me as curiously harsh and exaggerated, and its presence is especially ironic in a work which seeks to emphasize the values of objective scholarship.

My gratitude is due to Professor Harold Cherniss, without whose assistance it would have been totally impossible for me to have undertaken a study such as this, and to Professor I. M. Bocheński, for his friendly advice and encouragement.

Benson Mates

March 12, 1961

CONTENTS

Chapter I

INTRODUCTION

Summary

THE AIM of this study is to present a true description of the logic of the Old Stoa. It repeats most of Łukasiewicz's published conclusions on the subject and offers additional evidence for them. It also (1) describes the Stoic semantical theory and compares it with certain similar modern theories, (2) attempts to give a better account of the heretofore misunderstood Diodorean implication, (3) points out the Stoic version of the conditionalization principle, and (4) discusses the contention of the Stoics that their propositional logic was complete. In appendices it offers and justifies new translations of some important fragments pertaining to Stoic logic.

The Stoic authors in whose work we shall be interested primarily are Zeno, Cleanthes, and Chrysippus. Closely associated with them were Diodorus Cronus and Philo, of the Megarian school. Since the writings of these men have been lost, and since our sources usually do not distinguish between the views of the various Stoics, we are forced to treat the entire Old Stoa as a unit. This, of course, creates many difficulties. The best of our sources are Sextus Empiricus and Diocles Magnes (*apud* Diogenes Laertius). We also derive bits of information from Cicero, Gellius, Galen, Boethius, Apuleius, Alexander of Aphrodisias, Simplicius, Philoponus, Origen, Proclus, Stobaeus, Epictetus, Seneca, and a few others. Of these, only Epictetus and Seneca were favorably inclined toward Stoicism, and they, unfortunately, restricted their attention almost entirely to ethics. It is thus remarkable that the fragments of Stoic logic, transmitted by unsympathetic hands, are as clear and consistent as they are.

§ 1: The Problem

For more than two thousand years the logic of Aristotle exercised so complete a dominance over the field that in 1787 Immanuel Kant could say, "It is remarkable that to the present day it [logic] has not been able to make one step in advance, so that, to all appearance, it may be considered as completed and perfect."[1] But within fifty years after Kant's words were written there began a development which eventually succeeded in transforming logic into a discipline as exact and adequate as

---

[1] *Critique of Pure Reason*, trans. Max Müller (2d ed., New York, Macmillan, 1925), p. 688.

any part of mathematics. So many steps in advance have been made that the present-day student of logic is likely to find Aristotle mentioned only in the historical footnotes of his textbook.

The period of Aristotelian dominance in logic might well have ended sooner if certain ancient texts had been studied more carefully. About fifty years ago, C. S. Peirce noticed that the ancients had been aware of the relation now called "material implication" and had even carried on a great controversy over it.[2] So far as we know, neither Peirce nor anyone else pursued the subject further until 1927, when the eminent Polish logician Łukasiewicz pointed out that not only material implication but also many other important concepts and methods of modern logic had been anticipated in the writings of the early Stoics.[3] Łukasiewicz showed that Stoic logic had differed essentially from Aristotelian logic, with which it was later confused. The difference lay primarily in two circumstances: (1) Stoic logic was a logic of propositions, while Aristotelian logic was a logic of classes;[4] (2) Stoic logic was a theory of inference-

---

[2] *Collected Papers.* See vol. 2, p. 199, and vol. 3, pp. 279–280.

[3] For the most important writings of Łukasiewicz on Stoic logic, see the Bibliography.

[4] By characterizing Stoic logic as a logic of propositions and Aristotelian logic as a class logic, we mean that the values of the variables appearing in Stoic formulae are propositions (the substituends being sentences), while the values of Aristotelian variables are nonempty classes (the corresponding terms being the substituends). The Stoics used ordinal numerals as variables, whereas Aristotle and his followers used letters (Apuleius, *In De Interp.*, ed. Oud., 279; but cf. Galen, *Inst. Log.*, 15). The so-called "first undemonstrated" inference-schema of the Stoics ran as follows:

> If the first, then the second.
> The first.
> Therefore, the second.

As a concrete example of this type of inference, they were accustomed to give:

> If it is day, then it is light.
> It is day.
> Therefore, it is light.

Observe that the argument is obtained from the inference-schema by substituting the sentence, "It is day" for "the first," and "It is light" for "the second" throughout the schema. (See also Sextus, *Adv. Math.* VIII, 235 ff., 292; Origen, *Contra Celsum* VII, 15.) It *cannot* be obtained by substituting terms for the ordinal numerals. When the author of the Ammonian document (see Ammonius, *In An. Pr.*, p. 68, line 25) tried to make such a substitution he got:

> If man, then animal.
> But the first.
> Therefore, the second.

which is apparently intended to represent some such inference as this:

> For every x, if x is a man, then x is an animal.
> But a is a man.
> Therefore, a is an animal.

schemas, while Aristotelian logic was a theory of logically true matrices. Łukasiewicz showed also that the Stoics had used truth-functional definitions for all the common propositional connectives. He further drew attention to the fact that the Stoics clearly distinguished arguments from the corresponding conditional propositions, and, most important of all, that the Stoics had a kind of calculus of inference-schemas: they took five inference-schemas as valid without proof and rigorously derived other valid schemas from these. Comparing such facts with the extremely adverse and inaccurate characterizations of Stoic logic by Prantl, Zeller, and other "standard" authors, and observing that a similar situation obtained with respect to medieval logic, Łukasiewicz understandably came to the conclusion that the history of logic ought to be rewritten.

The present book attempts to give a reliable description of Stoic logic. It essays, therefore, only a small portion of the project suggested by Łukasiewicz. With a few minor exceptions it repeats his published conclusions and supports them with further evidence. In addition, it makes four points which are now summarized.

But this kind of inference is fundamentally different from that employed in the Stoic example.

Any doubt that the Stoic variables are propositional variables should be dispelled by the λογότροποι mentioned by Diogenes and Sextus:

> If Plato is living, then Plato is breathing.
> The first.
> Therefore, the second.

> If sweat flows through the surface, then the skin has intelligible pores.
> The first.
> Therefore, the second.

(Diog. L., *Vitae* VII, 77; Sextus, *Adv. Math.* VIII, 306. Cf. Sextus, *Hyp. Pyrrh.* II, 140.)

A typical Aristotelian syllogism is: If A belongs to all B, and C to all A, then C belongs to all B. (Aristotle, *An. Pr.*, 61b34. Aristotle himself stated *almost* all his syllogisms as conditionals, but the Peripatetics usually gave them as rules. See Bocheński, *De Consequentiis*, p. 7; Łukasiewicz, *Aristotle's Syllogistic*, pp. 1–3.) A concrete instance of this would be:

> If animal belongs to all ravens and substance to all animals, then substance belongs to all ravens.

Whether the foregoing is in need of appropriately placed quotation marks is a moot point, but in any case it is obvious that the result of substituting sentences for the variables in an Aristotelian syllogism will always be nonsensical.

Łukasiewicz ("Zur Geschichte der Aussagenlogik," p. 113) has noted the great confusion which is evident in Prantl's translation (*Geschichte der Logik*, vol. 1, p. 473) of the first Stoic schema:

> Wenn das Erste ist, ist das Zweite.
> Das Erste aber ja ist.
> Also ist das Zweite.

(R. D. Hicks, in the Loeb translation of Diogenes, vol. 2, p. 189, makes the same mistake.) Significantly, no counterpart of the word *ist* is to be found in the text which Prantl was translating. Cf. p. 70, note 53.

1. In their semantical theory the Stoics employed a distinction very similar to the sense-denotation and intension-extension distinctions of Frege and Carnap. Stoic logic is a logic of propositions and not of sentences.

2. Although the general outline of the Stoic controversy over the truth-conditions for "if . . . then" propositions is known well enough, certain important positions in the controversy have been greatly misunderstood. In particular, it has erroneously been supposed that the so-called "Diodorean implication" was an ancient version of strict implication. The present study offers a more faithful characterization of the view of Diodorus in regard to conditionals and shows how that view is closely connected with his rather unusual views on necessity and possibility. It also tries to give a more accurate account of the position of Chrysippus in the controversy, indicating that his type of implication was probably what is now known as "strict implication."

3. One of the Stoic principles noted by Łukasiewicz is clearly similar to modern theorems of great importance. This principle is as follows: an argument is valid if and only if the conditional proposition having the conjunction of the premises as antecedent and the conclusion as consequent is logically true. The similarity of this principle to the so-called "principle of conditionalization" and the "deduction theorem" is obvious but none the less interesting.

4. The Stoics maintained that their system of propositional logic was complete in the sense that every valid argument could be reduced to a series of arguments of five basic types. Even the method of reduction was not left vague, but was exactly characterized by four meta-rules, of which we possess two, and possibly three. Whether or not the Stoic system was actually complete could be decided only with the help of the missing rules.

Two appendices are included. Appendix A contains new translations of a number of the more important fragments pertaining to Stoic logic. Only such fragments are included as have not already been translated adequately into English; by this rule, however, nearly all the more important fragments are included. In the footnotes to these translations will be found various proposals for reconstructing portions of the texts of Sextus and Diogenes. Appendix B consists of a glossary of technical terms from Stoic logic. It is not intended primarily as a lexicon but rather as a convenient device for presenting evidence that indicates correct translations of the various terms concerned.

§ 2: STOIC AUTHORS TO BE CONSIDERED

Zeno, the founder of the Stoic school of philosophy, is said to have been influenced primarily by two of the Socratic schools, the Cynics and the Megarians.[5] From the Cynics, according to the usual account, he took his moral teaching; from the Megarians, his logic. In view of our present subject, we shall omit all discussion of the Cynics and devote our attention to the Megarians.

The Megarian school was founded by Euclid, a follower of Socrates and a somewhat older contemporary of Plato. (See fig. 1.) Among the

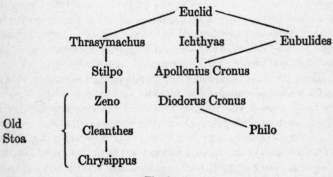

Fig. 1.

pupils of Euclid were: Eubulides, a famous logician to whom the antinomy of The Liar is sometimes ascribed; Ichthyas, the successor of Euclid as head of the school; and Thrasymachus of Corinth, who is known primarily as the teacher of Stilpo. Stilpo, a contemporary of Aristotle, enjoyed a great reputation as a lecturer. He is supposed to have been somewhat influenced by the Cynics. His most famous pupil was Zeno, founder of Stoicism. Another important branch of the Megarian school consisted of Eubulides, Apollonius Cronus, Diodorus Cronus, and Philo, in that order. The latter two are very important in connection with Stoic logic, mainly for their views on the truth-conditions of conditionals.

Diodorus, a native of Iasus in Caria, lived at the court of Alexandria in the reign of Ptolemy Soter. His surname or nickname "Cronus" ("old fool") is variously explained. According to one story, it was given to him by Ptolemy on account of his inability to solve a problem of logic put forth by Stilpo at a royal banquet. In fact, Diodorus is said to have taken

---

[5] For the following account I am indebted to Zeller, *Die Philosophie der Griechen*, vol. 2, part 1, pp. 244 ff., and vol. 3, part 1, pp. 27–49; W. Smith, *Dictionary of Greek and Roman Biography and Mythology* (Boston, Little, Brown, 1849), 3 vols.

his defeat so much to heart that he went home, wrote a treatise on the subject, and died in despair. According to another account, Diodorus took the surname from his teacher, Apollonius Cronus. At any rate, Diodorus was certainly not regarded as an old fool in antiquity. On the contrary, he was so celebrated for his dialectical skill that he was called "the logician" and "most logical one" (διαλεκτικώτατος). This epithet gradually became a surname, and was even applied to his five daughters, who were also distinguished as logicians.

Little is known of the philosophy of Diodorus save two important definitions (and examples illustrating these): (1) *a proposition is possible* if and only if it either is true or will be true; (2) *a conditional proposition is true* if and only if it neither is nor was possible for the antecedent to be true and the consequent false. It is known that he constructed the famous "Master" argument (ὁ κυριεύων) to justify his definition of "possible." It is also known that he entered into a controversy with his pupil Philo over the truth-conditions for hypothetical propositions; this controversy was perpetuated and enlarged within the Stoic school.[6]

Philo of Megara, the pupil of Diodorus, was also very famous as a logician. Almost nothing is reported of his life except that he was a friend of Zeno. Chrysippus later wrote treatises against both him and his master. Philo disagreed with Diodorus concerning the nature of possibility and especially concerning the criterion for the truth of conditional propositions. Regarding the first, he thought (as against Diodorus) that a piece of wood at the bottom of the sea should be considered combustible even if it will never be burned. In regard to conditionals, he gave exactly the modern truth-table definition: a conditional is false if it has a true antecedent and a false consequent; in the other three cases it is true.

Zeno himself apparently lived *ca.* 350–260 B.C., but the dates are very uncertain. Like all the other major Stoic philosophers before the Christian era, he was not a native of Greece proper. (His birthplace was at Citium, in Cyprus.) Few facts are known about him, but where the facts leave off, legend begins. It is said that he was greatly respected for his personal characteristics—dignity, modesty, sincerity, affability. Presumably because of a life of moderation, he lived to the ripe old age of ninety-eight, and, as the story has it, he died in the following way. As he was leaving the school one day, he stumbled and broke his toe. Beating his hand upon the ground, he addressed himself to the gods: "I'm coming of my own accord. Why then do you bother to call me?" Then he perished by holding his breath.

---

[6] The views of Diodorus will be discussed fully in the sequel, pp. 36–40, 44–51. Cf. my article, "Diodorean Implication."

Also according to the legends, Zeno devoted much thought and energy to proposed reforms in language. This aroused ire in certain quarters, and it was pointed out that he was proposing to reform a language which he himself could hardly speak. As he was fond of coining new words, much of the technical vocabulary of Stoic logic may well be attributed to him. It was said that he used new terms in order to conceal his plagiarism of the views of his predecessors; Cicero repeats this charge at least fourteen times. His writings, which were not numerous and were written in a very poor style, have been lost (excepting, of course, a few fragments).

The second head of the Stoic school was Cleanthes, known throughout antiquity as a man of strong character, great energy, and weak intellect. According to one story, he was a prize fighter who came to Athens with four drachmas in his pocket and entered the school of Zeno. He accepted Zeno's teaching in every detail and passed it on unchanged. At the age of ninety-nine or so, he died by starving himself to death.

Cleanthes was succeeded by Chrysippus, often said to have been the greatest logician of ancient times. Chrysippus was regarded as the second founder of Stoicism; according to an old saying, "If there had been no Chrysippus, there would have been no Stoa." He was born in 280 B.C. in Cilicia; the date of his death may be conjectured as 205 B.C. Without doubt, he was the best student his Stoic professors ever had. While in training, he thought of so many skeptical arguments against Stoicism that he was accused by the later Stoics of supplying Carneades with ammunition for attacking them. Chrysippus wrote 705 books, if the list given by Diogenes can be trusted. Of these we possess only the titles and a small number of fragments. But the titles alone show that he wrote on almost every important aspect of propositional logic. There are many ancient complaints that Chrysippus' books were dry and repetitious, and written in a very poor style. Yet they were widely read. He did not, like Cleanthes, merely repeat the words of his predecessors; there is a story that when he was a student of logic he wrote to Cleanthes, "Just send me the theorems. I'll find the proofs for myself."

It seems likely that Chrysippus was responsible for the final organization of Stoic logic into a calculus. When the five basic undemonstrated argument-types are cited, the name of Chrysippus is usually mentioned; in one place it is expressly stated that Chrysippus restricted the number of these types to five. At any rate, there is good reason to believe that, at least so far as logic is concerned, Zeller is near the truth when he states, "Aber die stoische Lehre hat durch Chrysippus ihre Vollendung erhalten;

als er um 206 v. Chr. starb, war die Gestalt, in welcher sie den folgenden Jahrhunderten überliefert wurde, nach allen Seiten hin festgestellt."[7]

§ 3: Sources for Stoic Logic

Except for a few fragments, all the writings of the earlier Stoics have been lost. We must therefore depend on secondary sources. But that is only half of the difficulty. Since none of the later Stoics had much to say about logic, we are in the very unsatisfactory position of having to depend on the accounts of men who were without exception opponents of the Stoics. In view of this, it is all the more remarkable that Stoic logic makes as excellent a showing as it does. Perhaps the saving circumstance was that the essentials of Stoic logic were brought together in handbooks not long after the time of Chrysippus. Such handbooks were commonly entitled "Introduction to Logic" (εἰσαγωγὴ διαλεκτική), and evidently had a very wide circulation. Whatever accuracy and sense remain in the bits of Stoic logic which have filtered down to us probably derive from the fact that our sources made use of the handbooks.

The difficulties created by the loss of the Stoic writings are even greater than might at first appear. Since our sources do not distinguish between the views of the various Stoics but rather tend to ascribe the sayings of any of them to all of them, we must treat the school as a whole, even though we know that this procedure will lead to apparent inconsistencies. Also, it is obvious that technical writings such as those on logic suffer from being reported at second hand; of all our sources, Sextus is the only one who seems to have had some understanding of the theory he was reporting. Another serious difficulty arises from the fact that our best sources are at least four hundred years later than Chrysippus. By this time the mixture and confusion of Stoic logic with that of Aristotle were well under way, producing strange conglomerates like that found in Galen's *Institutio Logica*. Since we do not possess the information necessary for disentangling the two doctrines, we can only make the best of it.

Far and away our most important source for Stoic logic is Sextus Empiricus, a Greek physician and Skeptic, who lived in the first half of the third century of the Christian era. Almost nothing is known of his life. Two of his works are extant, the *Outlines of Pyrrhonism*, in three books, and *Against the Mathematicians*, in eleven books. Most of his discussion of Stoic logic is to be found in Book II of the *Outlines* and Book VIII of *Against the Mathematicians;* the accounts given in these two places are often identical. Sextus is our only intelligent source. But even with him there is a fly in the ointment: he quotes the Stoics only to refute

[7] Zeller, *op. cit.*, vol. 3, part 1, p. 44.

them. We may expect, therefore, that any parts of Stoic logic which he found either too difficult or too good to refute will be absent from his account. Also, he emphasized those matters on which Stoic opinions differed, with the result that we get no clear statement of the logical doctrine of any one man.

The next best picture of Stoic logic is that given by Diogenes Laertius, author of *Lives of Eminent Philosophers*. There is no information whatever on his own life, but since Sextus and Saturninus are the latest writers he quotes, it is sometimes guessed that he lived in the third century of the Christian era. As is well known, Diogenes is wholly unreliable on many subjects. It is therefore fortunate for us that in writing his life of Zeno (Book VII) Diogenes had recourse to a book written by Diocles Magnes, a scholar of the first century B.C., who seems to have had a fair knowledge of Stoic logic. The most serious deficiency of Diogenes' account is its extreme brevity; what there is of it is as excellent as anything to be found in Sextus.

All our other sources for Stoic logic are relatively unsatisfactory. Scattered references to the Stoa will be found throughout the twenty volumes of Galen's works,[8] but discussions of any extent are rare. The little treatise called *Historia Philosopha* contains the remains of a good account of the five basic undemonstrated argument-types. However, it has been necessary for editors to reconstruct the text on the analogy of corresponding passages in Sextus; consequently it has little independent value. There is also the handbook, *Institutio Logica*, ascribed to Galen by the manuscripts. Prantl has vehemently challenged its authenticity; Kalbfleisch has "proved" it genuine with equal vigor.[9] In any case, the treatise is of considerable interest to historians of logic. Although it is a mixture of Aristotelian and Stoic logic, its account of the five basic types of argument is clear and agrees exactly with our other information. Its criticism of these, however, is typically Peripatetic and typically confused. The treatise contains a few further hints about the views of the Stoics, but nothing else of value for our purpose.

Other scraps of information are to be found in the writings of Cicero, Gellius, and the many Aristotelian commentators.[10] Most of these scraps

[8] The best exegetical study of the logic of Galen is by Stakelum, *Galen and the Logic of Propositions*. See especially the summary, pp. 90–91.

[9] Prantl, *op. cit.*, pp. 591–610; Kalbfleisch, "Ueber Galens Einleitung in die Logik," pp. 681–708.

[10] The relevant writings of these authors are listed in the Bibliography. An excellent critical discussion of Apuleius, Alexander of Aphrodisias, Sextus, Diogenes Laertius, Themistius, Boethius, Ammonius, Simplicius, and Philoponus as sources of information about ancient logic may be found in Bocheński, *La Logique de Théophraste*, chap. i.

fit consistently into the picture, but they are too brief to be of much help. The work of the later Aristotelian commentators reveals extreme confusion between Stoic and Aristotelian logic, and hence is of very little use as a source.

All our sources have one characteristic in common: the more interesting the logic becomes, the more corrupt the text becomes. Because of the technical terminology and the very unusual sentences with which the Stoics sometimes illustrated their points, the origin of these textual difficulties is understandable—but the difficulties remain. Especially is this noticeable in Galen's *Institutio Logica*, where occasionally the whole thread of argument is lost.

In view of all these difficulties, the reader may well wonder whether there is enough evidence to justify the attempt to give a complete account of Stoic logic. He may answer this question for himself by reading the following chapters and, if he is interested, by checking the exposition against the Stoic passages which are cited. He will find that no effort has been made to conceal or minimize evidence contrary to the various theses proposed; the price exacted by this procedure is that the account is not always as simple and clear as one might desire.

CHAPTER II

SIGNS, SENSE, AND DENOTATION

SUMMARY

THE CHAPTER is divided into two sections. The first contains an account of the Stoic distinction between the sign, the significate (called the "Lekton"), and the physical object to which the sign refers. Various types of signs and their corresponding Lekta are described in detail. In the second section the Stoic theory is compared with the modern theories of Frege and Carnap and is shown to bear marked resemblance to them, particularly in regard to what Carnap calls the "intension" of linguistic expressions. Numerous dissimilarities are also indicated, the most important of which are: (1) the Stoics restricted the denotation of expressions to *bodies*; (2) the Stoics did not take truth-values as the denotations of sentences.

§ 1: EXPOSITION OF THE STOIC THEORY

Three things, according to the Stoics, are connected with one another: (1) the significans, or sign; (2) the significate; and (3) that which exists.[1] The significans is the sound, for example, the sound "Dion." That which exists is the externally existing object, which in the same example would be Dion himself.[2] These two—the sound and that which exists—are bodies, or physical objects. The third factor, however, is not a body. It is described as "the actual entity[3] indicated or revealed by the sound and which we apprehend as subsisting together with [i.e., in] our thought."[4] It is what the Barbarians do not understand when they hear Greek words spoken.[5] The Stoic technical name for it is λεκτόν, which may be translated literally as "that which is meant."[6]

These three factors are distinguished also in an example given by

---

[1] Sextus, *Adv. Math.* VIII, 11 ff. οἱ ἀπὸ τῆς Στοᾶς τρία φάμενοι συζυγεῖν ἀλλήλοις, τό τε σημαινόμενον καὶ τὸ σημαῖνον καὶ τὸ τυγχάνον.

[2] *Ibid.*, 12. αὐτὸς ὁ Δίων.

[3] I use "entity" for τὸ πρᾶγμα here, as I can find no better word. "Thing" often connotes physicality and thus would be quite unsuitable.

[4] *Adv. Math.* VIII, 12. σημαινόμενον δὲ αὐτὸ τὸ πρᾶγμα τὸ ὑπ' αὐτῆς δηλούμενον καὶ οὗ ἡμεῖς μὲν ἀντιλαμβανόμεθα τῇ ἡμετέρᾳ παρυφισταμένου διανοίᾳ.

[5] *Ibid.* Cf. I, 37, 155.

[6] In Stoic terminology, λέγειν was distinguished from προστάττειν. λέγειν was "to utter a sound signifying the thought" (*Adv. Math.* VIII, 80). The meaning of προστάττειν is distinguished as in the following passage: ὁ γὰρ λέγων Μὴ κλέψῃς, λέγει μὲν αὐτὸ τοῦτο, Μὴ κλέψῃς, προστάσσει δὲ μὴ κλέπτειν (Plutarch, *De Stoic. Repugn.*, chap. 11, p. 1037d). Cf. however, Steinthal, *Geschichte der Sprachwissenschaft*, vol. 1, p. 293, on the difference between λέγειν and προφέρεσθαι.

Seneca.[7] Suppose, he says, that I see Cato walking. The sense of sight
discloses this to me; the mind believes it. That which I see, and to which
I direct my eyes and my mind, is a body. But when I say, "Cato is
walking" (the sound), what I mean (the Lekton) is not a body but rather
a certain affirmation *about* a body. Some call it "affirmation"; some call
it "proposition"; and some, "assertion." There is a great deal of difference, Seneca observes, between what I mean (the Lekton) and what I
am talking *about* (the body).

Again, as Diogenes tells us, speech is very different from mere utterance, for only sounds are uttered, but matters of discourse (τὰ πράγματα)
are spoken of, and these are really Lekta.[8]

There is little doubt that this distinction represents a fundamental,
though debated, part of Stoic theory. Accordingly, we are told in many
places[9] that Chrysippus divided logic into two parts, one having to do
with signs (τὰ σημαίνοντα) and one dealing with significates (τὰ σημαινόμενα). But there is also little doubt that however clear these distinctions may originally have been, much confusion surrounded them in
later centuries, especially in the minds of the Aristotelian commentators.
For example, Ammonius[10] says that the Lekton of the Stoics is an intermediate entity between the thought and the thing, but in Simplicius[11] we
read that Lekta and thoughts are identical. The confusion is augmented
by Philoponus, Themistius, and the Ammonian document, which all say
that the Stoics called things τυγχάνοντα, thoughts ἐκφορικά, and sounds
λεκτά (Lekta).[12] There seems to be no doubt that Philoponus and
Themistius are mistaken, as Zeller supposed;[13] the corresponding passage
in the Ammonian document, not mentioned by Zeller, is of course just
as mistaken. The statement by Ammonius is incompatible with that of
Simplicius; hence one of these must be rejected, too. That both of them
may be in error is suggested by the following passage in Galen:

Since we have memories of things that are perceived by the senses, whenever we set
these in motion they are to be called by the term νόησις [thought]; but whenever they

---

[7] *Ep.*, 117, 13.
[8] Diog. L., *Vitae* VII, 57 (cf. also note 51). It should be observed that throughout
these discussions (Sextus, *Adv. Math.* VIII, 11–12; Diog. L., *Vitae* VII, 57) τὸ πρᾶγμα
refers to what is signified, i.e., to the Lekton. (See Steinthal, *op. cit.*, p. 288.) Prantl,
by overlooking this, gives a contradictory account (*Geschichte der Logik im Abendland*,
vol. 1, pp. 415–416) of Lekta, stating first that they are τὰ πράγματα (*die Dinge*) and
then that they are *not* "*die Dinge.*"
[9] Seneca, *Ep.*, 89, 17; Diog. L., *Vitae* VII, 43, 62.
[10] Ammonius, *In De Interp.*, ed. Busse, p. 17, line 27.
[11] Simplicius, *In Cat.*, ed. Kalbfleisch, p. 11, line 4.
[12] Ioannes Philoponus, *In An. Pr.*, ed. Wallies, pp. 243 ff.; Themistius, *In An. Pr.*,
ed. Wallies, p. 92, line 3; Ammonius, *In An. Pr.*, ed. Wallies, p. 68, lines 4 ff.
[13] Zeller, *Die Philosophie der Griechen*, vol. 3, part 1, pp. 88–89, note 2.

happen to be silent, they are to be called ἔννοιαι [notions]. There are also some further notions which do not arise from sense perception but are naturally in all of us, and when these are expressed in sound, the ancient philosophers call them by the term ἀξίωμα [proposition]. The Greeks, to be sure, often call notions "thoughts."[14]

Even Sextus' account of the Stoic theory of signs contains a radical difficulty which seems to have been overlooked by all the authors who have discussed the point (with the notable exception of Sextus himself). Sextus tells us that the sign (τὸ σημαῖνον), as contrasted with the significate (τὸ λεκτόν), is a material object. As we shall see later, propositions (ἀξιώματα) are defined as constituting one species of Lekton, and thus are not physical objects; therefore, this account does not represent signs as propositions. Nevertheless, after explaining that the Stoics divided signs (τὰ σημεῖα) into two kinds, commemorative and indicative, Sextus says that indicative signs, according to the Stoics, are antecedent propositions in certain types of true conditionals.[15] This would imply that indicative signs are propositions. I do not know how to explain this difficulty.[16]

The Stoic distinction of signals (let us now adopt this translation for σημεῖον) into commemorative and indicative is itself of some interest. According to Sextus, the term "signal" has two senses, a common sense and a special sense. In its common usage the word refers to anything which, as it were, serves to "reveal" something else which has previously been observed in conjunction with it. In the special sense it means that which is indicative of something nonevident (τὸ ἐνδεικτικὸν τοῦ ἀδηλουμέ-νου πράγματος).[17] Signals, in the former sense of the word, are called "commemorative"; in the latter, "indicative."[18] Thus the commemorative signal, having been observed in a clear perception together with the object signified, makes us remember that which was observed along with it, when the object signified is not evident.[19] For example, we have

[14] Galen, *Inst. Log.*, ed. Kalbfleisch, p. 7, line 22, to p. 8, line 7. A proposition (ἀξίωμα) is a sort of Lekton.

[15] Sextus, *Adv. Math.* VIII, 245. See the Glossary, s.v. ἀληθής.

[16] Of the many possible explanations, a few are as follows. (1) Perhaps in technical Stoic language, τὸ σημαῖνον and τὸ σημεῖον are not synonymous. The fact that only τὸ σημεῖον is used in the passages defining signs as antecedent propositions in certain conditionals, while only τὸ σημαῖνον is used in the passages distinguishing the sign from the Lekton, lends some evidence to this hypothesis. (2) Perhaps one or more of the foregoing terms had two senses in Stoic logic. As the example of "truth" shows (see chap. iii), there would be a good deal of precedent for this. (3) Possibly the in-consistent accounts refer to different Stoic writers or represent a mixture of Stoicism with something else. This possibility is not at all improbable, since our sources for Stoic doctrine frequently attribute the views of any Stoic to all Stoics and, further, do not always make it plain where their expositions of Stoicism begin and where they end.

[17] Sextus. *Adv. Math.* VIII, 143

[18] *Ibid.*, 151.

[19] *Ibid.*, 152.

many times observed smoke and fire in conjunction. Consequently, when we see smoke we immediately recall the (presently unseen) fire. The same relations hold, we are informed, in the case of the scar which follows the wound, and in the case of death following rupture of the heart; for when we see the scar, we recall the antecedent wound, and seeing the rupture of the heart, we foretell the impending death.[20]

The indicative signal, on the contrary, can never be observed in connection with the object signified, since what is not observable is a fortiori not observable in connection with something else.[21] The soul is an example of something that is naturally nonevident, for it never presents itself to our clear perception. Nevertheless, it is indicated, or signified indicatively, by the bodily motions. For we "reason" that the body has a kind of internal power to manifest such motions.[22]

To return for a moment to the difficulty mentioned above, we may observe that the entire discussion of signals, down to this point, is compatible with the view that they are physical objects. However, in his attempt to prove that these distinctions are worthless, Sextus considers two possibilities: either the indicative signals are sensible objects or they are not. In connection with the latter possibility he states, ". . . thus the Stoics, who appear to have defined it [the signal] exactly, attempting to establish the concept of the signal, say that a signal is a true antecedent proposition in a true conditional and is such that it serves to reveal the consequent."[23] He then goes on to define proposition; and of the term προκαθηγούμενον, which I have translated as "true antecedent," he says, "By προκαθηγούμενον they mean the antecedent of a true conditional which has a true antecedent and a true consequent. It serves to reveal the consequent; for instance, the proposition 'She has milk' serves to reveal the proposition 'She has conceived' in this conditional: 'If she has milk, then she has conceived.' "[24]

Sextus then tries to show that there is no evidence for the existence of any such thing as a Lekton and that therefore there is no evidence for the existence of any such thing as a προκαθηγούμενον. This indicates that Sextus, if he is honest, believes himself to be refuting a Stoic view which holds that indicative signals are not physical objects but rather Lekta—specifically, propositions. But at the same time he makes statements such as the following: "We have shown many times and in many places that some things signify and others are signified. Sounds signify, while

[20] *Ibid.*, 153.
[21] *Ibid.*, 154.
[22] *Ibid.*, 155.
[23] Sextus, *Hyp. Pyrrh.* II, 104; cf. *Adv. Math.* VIII, 245.
[24] *Hyp. Pyrrh.* II, 106.

the things signified are Lekta, which include propositions. And since all propositions are things signified and not things signifying, it follows that the signal [τὸ σημεῖον] will not be a proposition."[25] Thus Sextus himself points out the contradiction which we have been considering.

We cannot attribute the doctrine of Lekta to the Stoics without certain reservations. There seems to have been a dispute within the school itself whether any such things existed. This, however, is hardly surprising, since, so far as we know, the prevailing Stoic metaphysical view was pansomatism, the view that only bodies exist.[26] Sextus tells us that some have denied the existence of the Lekta and that these are not only men of other schools—for example, the Epicureans—but also some of the Stoics themselves.[27] For instance, Basileides and his followers held that nothing incorporeal exists.[28] Later, Sextus mentions that the battle over the existence of the Lekta is unending.[29]

The Stoic definition of Lekton, as reported by Sextus and Diogenes in almost identical passages, is "that which subsists in conformity with a rational presentation."[30] Sextus goes on to say that according to the Stoics a rational presentation is one in which the φαντασθέν (that which is presented) can be conveyed by discourse (λόγῳ). Later, he tells us that "to say something, as the Stoics themselves declare, is to utter a sound

[25] *Adv. Math.* VIII, 264. See *ibid.*, 11, where this view is expressly attributed to the Stoics.

[26] Zeller, *op. cit.*, vol. 3, part 1, p. 119, note 2, gives many references for this.

[27] *Adv. Math.* VIII, 258.

[28] Basileides was a teacher of Marcus Aurelius, according to Zeller; Brochard supposes that he is the Stoic listed in *Index Hercul.* C. 51.

[29] *Adv. Math.* VIII, 262; I, 28. With reference to this matter Zeller says, "Doch waren es wahrscheinlich erst jüngere Stoïker, welche, von ihren Gegnern gedrängt, diesen Zweifel erhoben: Basilides war der Lehrer Mark Aurels; sonst aber wird ganz unbefangen von dem Sein der λεκτά gesprochen" (*op. cit.*, vol. 3, part 1, p. 89, note 1). Scholz, however, says that Chrysippus himself materialized propositions and that the Peripatetic reaction to this is at the root of Galen's whole account of logic (*Deutsche Literaturzeitung*, nos. 37–38 [1941], cols. 866–869). Indeed, there are a number of passages like the following (from Galen): "The followers of Chrysippus, fixing their attention more on the speech than on the objects, use the term 'conjunction' for all propositions compounded by means of the conjunctive connectives . . ." (*Inst. Log.*, p. 11, lines 5 ff.) ". . . such a statement as this: 'If it is not day, then it is night,' which, when it is said in a conditional form of speech, is called a 'conditional' by those who pay attention only to the sounds, but a 'disjunction' by those who pay attention to what is meant" (*ibid.*, p. 9, lines 11 ff.). These passages, however, do not say that Chrysippus identified propositions with sentences or sounds. Apparently the Peripatetics wished to argue that logically equivalent propositions were identical (e.g., "If it is not day, then it is night" and "Either it is day or it is night"), whereas the Stoic view was that propositions were structurally isomorphic to their corresponding sentences.

[30] Sextus, *Adv. Math.* VIII, 70: λεκτὸν δὲ ὑπάρχειν φασὶ τὸ κατὰ λογικὴν φαντασίαν ὑφιστάμενον, λογικὴν δὲ εἶναι φαντασίαν καθ' ἣν τὸ φαντασθὲν ἔστι λόγῳ παραστῆσαι. Diog. L., *Vitae* VII, 63: φασὶ δὲ τὸ λεκτὸν εἶναι τὸ κατὰ φαντασίαν λογικὴν ὑφιστάμενον. *Ibid.*, 51: Ἔτι τῶν φαντασιῶν αἱ μέν εἰσι λογικαί, αἱ δὲ ἄλογοι· λογικαὶ μὲν αἱ τῶν λογικῶν ζῴων, ἄλογοι δὲ αἱ τῶν ἀλόγων. αἱ μὲν οὖν λογικαὶ νοήσεις εἰσίν, αἱ δ' ἄλογοι οὐ τετυχήκασιν ὀνόματος.

capable of signifying the object conceived."[31] All these remarks, unfortunately, leave us pretty much in the dark about the meaning of Lekta.
However, a survey of the extension of the term is helpful. Both Sextus
and Diogenes, again in almost identical passages, say that the Stoics
divide Lekta into two kinds: those that are complete in themselves and
those that are deficient.[32] Deficient Lekta are described as "those the

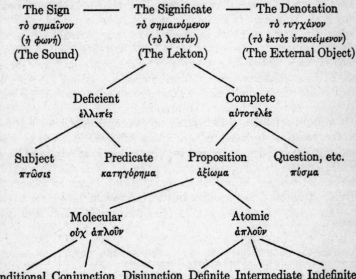

Fig. 2.

enunciation of which is incomplete, for example, 'writes'—for we want
to know 'who?' "[33] Complete Lekta are those having complete enunciation. Further examples will be given in the sequel.

Deficient Lekta are divided into two classes, πτώσεις and κατηγορήματα.[34]

[31] *Adv. Math.* VIII, 80.
[32] *Ibid.*, 70: τῶν δὲ λεκτῶν τὰ μὲν ἐλλιπῆ καλοῦσι, τὰ δὲ αὐτοτελῆ. See figure 2 for a rep-
resentation of the entire classification. Cf. Diog. L., *Vitae* VII, 63; see also von Arnim,
Stoicorum Veterum Fragmenta, vol. 2, p. 182. The latter is hereafter cited as *SVF*.
[33] *Vitae* VII, 63.
[34] See Zeller, *op. cit.*, vol. 3, part 1, p. 90, note 2., for a discussion of this point.
Zeller's discussion, however, is seriously confused. He does not notice, for example,
that at Diog. L., *Vitae* VII, 58, which is cited by him, the ῥῆμα is said to *signify* the
κατηγόρημα, whereas at Plutarch, *Qu. Plat.* X, 1,2, p. 1009c, also cited by him, the ῥῆμα
is said to *be* the κατηγόρημα. Then Zeller himself says that the incomplete Lekta (which,
of course, are *not* corporeal) are divided into proper names and adjectives (*Eigen-
schaftswörter*). The entire matter is clouded by all the conflicting testimony; I have
followed Diogenes, who at least gives an internally consistent account. Very likely,

It is difficult to translate these terms exactly, partly because of conflicting ancient testimony and partly because they are technical and most of
the various possible English translations for them are also technical. But
the following points may help to establish their meaning. Among the
parts of speech, which are signs and hence physical objects, there are
proper names (ὀνόματα), class names (προσηγορίαι), and verbs (ῥήματα).[35]
A proper name—"Diogenes," "Socrates," "Paris," "Achilles"—is a part
of speech which signifies a *quality* which belongs to one individual at
most.[36] Note that "signifies" is here used to indicate the relation between
the sign and the Lekton. A class name is a part of speech which signifies
a *common* quality: "man," "horse," "goddess," "soothsayer," "wrath."[37]
(I use "quality" as a translation for ποιότης; however, ποιότης carries a
reference to the sort of thing concerned, and hence has a meaning which
overlaps that of "quality.") A verb (this, again, may be too narrow a
translation of ῥῆμα) is a part of speech which signifies an uncompounded
κατηγόρημα: "to drink absinth," "to sit," "to walk," "to sing."[38] We may
thus translate κατηγόρημα as "predicate," if it is understood that in this
usage "predicate" does not denote a sign or any other physical object;[39]
and perhaps the best translation of πτῶσις will be "subject"; it is a
generic term for those entities expressed by individual names or class
names.[40] Therefore, as we are told by Diogenes, a predicate is a deficient
Lekton which combines with a subject (in the nominative case) to form
a proposition.[41] So, for example, the words "walks" and "sits" express
predicates.

much of the confusion in these matters derives from the fact that in Aristotelian logic
a proposition is composed of a noun and a verb (words). Cf. Apuleius, *In De Interp.*,
ed. Oud., 267; Aristotle, *De Interp.*, 5.

[35] Diog. L., *Vitae* VII, 57 ff.; Galen, *De Hipp. et Plat. Plac.* VIII, 3; Sextus, *Adv.
Math.* I, 132.

[36] Diog. L., *Vitae* VII, 58: ὄνομα δέ ἐστι μέρος λόγου δηλοῦν ἰδίαν ποιότητα. See also
Scholia in Dionysii Thracis Artem Grammaticum, ed. Hilgard, 214; and Sextus, *Adv.
Math.* I, 133.

[37] Diog. L., *Vitae* VII, 58: Ἔστι δὲ προσηγορία μὲν κατὰ τὸν Διογένην μέρος λόγου
σημαῖνον κοινὴν ποιότητα, οἷον Ἄνθρωπος, Ἵππος. Cf. also Sextus, *Adv. Math.* I, 133.

[38] *Vitae* VII, 58: ῥῆμα δέ ἐστι μέρος λόγου σημαῖνον ἀσύνθετον κατηγόρημα. For the examples
see Sextus, *Hyp. Pyrrh.* II, 230, 232; *Adv. Math.* VIII, 100, and I, 133. Steinthal, *op.
cit.*, p. 299, asserts that ῥῆμα = κατηγόρημα—an amazing assertion in view of the fact
that we are told by Diogenes (1) that a ῥῆμα *signifies* (σημαίνει) a κατηγόρημα, and (2)
that a ῥῆμα is a φωνή (hence, a σῶμα), whereas a κατηγόρημα is a Lekton (hence,
ἀσώματον).

[39] This agrees with Frege's usage of *Prädikat*. Cf. Sextus, *Adv. Math.* VIII, 100,
where a κατηγόρημα may "belong" to an object.

[40] Thus, the sound "dog" signifies (σημαίνει) a πτῶσις—e.g., a barking animal. *Adv.
Math.* XI, 29.

[41] Diog. L., *Vitae* VII, 64. A predicate is a λεκτὸν ἐλλιπὲς συντακτὸν ὀρθῇ πτώσει πρὸς
ἀξιώματος γένεσιν. Cf. also Sextus, *Adv. Math.* VIII, 79, 94. I do not understand how
a Lekton, as distinguished from a word, can possibly be in the nominative case. But
there are many things about the metaphysics of Lekta, as also of propositions, which
I do not understand. This applies especially to the assertion that Lekta and propositions have parts (μόρια).

At this point, under the heading "deficient Lekta," we should expect to find accounts of the famous Stoic theory of categories. But we do not, and, as Zeller points out, there is nothing on record to indicate where the discussion of the categories occurred in Stoic introductions to logic.[42] Furthermore, there is almost no consideration of the categories in Sextus, Diogenes Laertius, or Galen, who are our only good sources for Stoic logic. Instead, we have to depend on Alexander, Simplicius, Dexippus, Porphyry, Plutarch, and Stobaeus, with certain hints by Seneca and others, all of whom we know to be relatively unreliable in such matters.[43] We shall consequently restrict the present account to the barest outline of the Stoic categories, hoping that others will be able to investigate this matter more successfully in the future.

Compared with Aristotle's ten categories, those of the Stoics number only four, plus one "highest notion." The highest notion was called τὸ τί, "the indefinite something," and the four categories were:

(1)	τὸ ὑποκείμενον	subject or substratum
(2)	τὸ ποιόν	quality
(3)	τὸ πως ἔχον	state
(4)	τὸ πρὸς τί πως ἔχον	relation

We are told that these four categories are so related to one another that every preceding category is contained in and more accurately determined by the next succeeding one.[44] De Lacy[45] claims to discern, in the writings of Epictetus and others, actual attempts to investigate subjects by means of the categories. Epictetus, in discussing some matter, will first state the subject, then its qualities, then its states, and so on. Since, however, De Lacy has found no example in which all four categories are used, and since it would obviously be very difficult to treat any subject without using at least some of them, it seems that his thesis is at present insufficiently supported by evidence.

We turn now to the complete Lekta. For logic, the most important subclass of these is that consisting of propositions. A proposition, according to the standard Stoic definition, is a complete Lekton that is assertoric (i.e., true or false) in itself.[46] But there are also many other kinds of complete Lekta.[47] There are questions, which, like propositions, are

---

[42] Zeller, *op. cit.*, vol. 3, part 1, p. 92, note 1. Cf. Bocheński, *Ancient Formal Logic*, p. 87.

[43] For sources see Zeller, *op. cit.*, vol. 3, part 1, pp. 93 ff.

[44] *Ibid.*, p. 104.

[45] "Stoic Categories as Methodological Principles," pp. 246–263.

[46] Sextus, *Adv. Math.* VIII, 73, 74; Diog. L., *Vitae* VII, 65; Gellius, *Noctes Atticae* XVI, viii.

[47] *Adv. Math.* VIII, 71 ff.; *Vitae* VII, 66 ff. Cf. also Apuleius, *In De Interp.*, ed. Oud., p. 265; and *SVF* II, 182.

complete Lekta, but which demand an answer: "Is it day?" These are neither true nor false. There are inquiries, which are like questions except that they cannot be answered with "Yes" or "No": "Where does Dion live?" (Here, in parallel accounts, Sextus gives the question and Diogenes gives the answer: "He lives at such and such a place.") There are imperatives (which convey commands), oaths, and salutations ('Ατρεΐδη κύδιστε, ἄναξ ἀνδρῶν 'Αγάμεμνον). Besides these, there are quasi-questions ("How like to Priam's sons the cowherd is!"), and timid suggestions, and wishes, and prayers, and many others.

Such is the classification of Lekta. Since we are dealing with logic we shall be interested primarily in only one sort of complete Lekton, the proposition. This will be considered in the next chapter.

§ 2: COMPARISON WITH MODERN THEORIES

There are interesting similarities between Stoic semantics and certain modern theories, particularly those of Frege and Carnap. The goal here, as elsewhere in this study, is to give a true picture of the Stoic contributions and not to try to show that there is nothing new under the sun. For Frege's theory we shall rely on a long-neglected article[48] which is the source of many of the examples and much of the substance found in the contemporary discussions among Carnap, Quine, Church, and others. Carnap's view will be taken from one of his recent books,[49] which, conveniently for the present task, contains a comparison of his intension-extension distinction with Frege's distinction between sense and denotation.[50] The traditional concepts of the connotation, denotation, extension, and intension of terms are subsumed as special cases under the much wider concepts introduced by Frege and Carnap, which apply to whole sentences as well as to their parts. It will be seen below that the Stoic theory is also of the wider rather than of the narrower sort; this is why Frege and Carnap were chosen for comparison instead of one of the traditional authors, for instance, Mill.[51]

---

[48] Frege, "Ueber Sinn und Bedeutung," pp. 25–50.

[49] Carnap, *Meaning and Necessity.*

[50] I shall adopt the following translations of Frege's terms:

Sinn: sense	*Zeichen:* sign
Bedeutung: denotation	*Bezeichnen:* designate
Bedeuten: denote	*Gegenstand:* object
Ausdrücken: express	*Subjekt:* subject
Gedanke: proposition	*Prädikat:* predicate
Vorstellung: idea	*Behauptungssatz:* sentence

Cf. Carnap, *op. cit.,* p. 118, note 21. The term *Eigenname* is introduced by Frege (*op. cit.,* p. 27) to refer to names of individuals, but he does not adhere closely to this usage (cf. p. 34).

[51] Cf. Brochard, "Sur la logique des Stoïciens," p. 465.

TABLE 1
Comparison of Stoic Terminology with That of Frege and Carnap

	Signs			Sense			Denotation		
	1	2	3	4	5	6	7	8	9
a	τὸ σημαῖνον	Zeichen	Designator	τὸ λεκτόν	Sinn	Intension	τὰ σώματα	Bedeutung	Extension
b	τὸ ὄνομα	Eigenname	Individual expression	ἡ ἰδία ποιότης	Subjekt	Individual concept		Gegenstände ("in the widest sense")	Individual
c	ἡ προσηγορία	No specific term used	Class name	ἡ κοινὴ ποιότης	Subjekt	Property			Class
d	τὸ ῥῆμα	No specific term used	Predicate	τὸ κατηγόρημα	Prädikat	Property			Class
e	ὁ λόγος	Behauptungssatz	Sentence	τὸ ἀξίωμα	Gedanke	Proposition		Wahrheitswerth	Truth-value

In order to simplify discussion and comparison of the three sets of concepts, table 1 has been adjoined. It consists of an arrangement of the corresponding terms employed in the three theories, and references will be made to it by row and column. Columns 1, 4, and 7 contain Stoic terms; columns 2, 5, and 8, Frege's terms; columns 3, 6, and 9, Carnap's terms.

At the outset we must mention two serious deficiencies in the Stoic theory (or in what remains of it), compared with the theories of Frege and Carnap. In the first place, no principle of interchangeability is to be found in any of the Stoic fragments, nor is there any discussion of the problems which arise in connection with such a principle.[52] We have only the bare essentials of the Stoic theory; there are no examples of the application of their principles to the solution of definite problems. Thus, the attempt to solve the so-called "antinomy of the name-relation," which in one form or another has set the tenor of the modern approaches, is wholly absent from what little Stoic theory has filtered down to us.[53] Second, and closely associated with the same point, is the fact that we possess no Stoic discussions of "oblique"[54] or "not purely designative"[55] occurrences of linguistic expressions. Owing to this fact, it will be possible for us to compare what is known of the Stoic concepts with the concepts of Frege and Carnap much more simply than might at first appear. For, as Carnap says, his concepts coincide with those of Frege for ordinary occurrences of expressions: for any expression, its ordinary sense and its ordinary denotation are, respectively, the same as its intension and its extension.[56] Therefore, we have no basis for discussing the Stoic theory in any respect in which the theories of Carnap and Frege do not coincide.

The fundamental Stoic distinction is that between τὸ σημαῖνον, τὸ λεκτόν, and τὸ τυγχάνον. This corresponds, in many respects, to the

---

[52] Leibniz' statement of the principle, quoted by Frege (*op. cit.*, p. 35), is "Eadem sunt quae sibi mutuo substitui possunt, salva veritate." Cf. Carnap, *op. cit.*, pp. 51 ff., 121–122. Cf. also Sextus, *Hyp. Pyrrh.* II, 227: "Just as, because Paris and Alexander are identical, it is not possible for 'Alexander walks' to be true and 'Paris walks' to be false. . . ." The context suggests that Sextus thought that the Stoics would agree to this—possibly because it was an application of one of their own principles. "Paris" and "Alexander" were standard Stoic examples. Cf. Simplicius, *In Cat.*, ed. Kalbfleisch, p. 36, lines 8 ff.

[53] Cf. Carnap, *op. cit.*, pp. 133 ff. We do know, however, that the Epicureans, against whom the Stoics primarily contended, held the naïve sign-object view which gives rise to the antinomy (Sextus, *Adv. Math.* VIII, 13). We know also that Chrysippus proposed certain paradoxes requiring a notion of sense for their easy solution: e.g., "Dion has died." (If the sentence is true, there is no denotation for "Dion"; yet the sentence is significant.)

[54] Frege, *op. cit.*, pp. 28 *et passim*.

[55] W. V. Quine, "Notes on Existence and Necessity," *Journal of Philosophy*, vol. 40 (1943), pp. 113–127.

[56] Carnap, *op. cit.*, p. 126.

Zeichen-Sinn-Bedeutung and designator-intension-extension distinctions
of Frege and Carnap. That the concepts of τὸ σημαῖνον, *Zeichen*, and
designator coincide, there is no doubt. With regard to τὸ λεκτόν, *Sinn*, and
intension, however, the agreement is not complete.

The Lekton is that which the sign designates or means, and which we
grasp (ἀντιλαμβανόμεθα) as existing in close connection with our intellect;
again, it is what the Barbarians do not understand when they hear the
Greek words spoken.[57] The concepts of *Sinn* and intension, according
to Carnap, "refer to meaning in a strict sense, as that which is grasped
when we understand an expression without knowing the facts."[58] Frege
explains the sense of a sign as "the manner in which that which is denoted
by the sign is given." For instance, he says, let *a*, *b*, *c* be the medians of a
triangle. Then "the intersection of *a* and *b*" denotes the same point as
"the intersection of *b* and *c*," but the two expressions do not have the
same sense.[59] "Morning star" and "evening star" are another pair of
expressions which have the same denotation but different senses.

Frege carefully differentiates between the idea (*Vorstellung*) and the
sense.[60] The idea, he says, is subjective and private; the sense is objective
and public. Similarly, the Stoics distinguished between the presentation
(φαντασία) and the Lekton. The latter is that which is the content of a
rational presentation, which in turn is a presentation with respect to
which the φαντασθέν can be conveyed by discourse.[61] That is, the Lekton
is what might be called the "objective content" (τὸ φαντασθέν) of the
presentation, whereas the sense is characterized by Frege as the "objective content" of the *Vorstellung*.[62] Again, Frege describes the sense as
being "between" the subjective idea and the denoted object;[63] this is
parallel to Ammonius' description of the Lekton as a μέσον between
the thought (νόημα) and the thing (τὸ πρᾶγμα).[64]

These general descriptions of Lekton and sense show a certain similarity, so far as they are intelligible. But a judgment about the coincidence or noncoincidence of the two would hardly be trustworthy if it
were based only on characterizations so vague as these. What we need
to know is this: Is the Lekton of every expression the same as its (ordi-

---

[57] Sextus, *Adv. Math.* VIII, 12, 70.
[58] Carnap, *op. cit.*, p. 119.
[59] Frege, *op. cit.*, pp. 26–27.
[60] *Ibid.*, pp. 30 ff.
[61] Sextus, *Adv. Math.* VIII, 70.
[62] In fact, Zeller's translation of φαντασία is *Vorstellung*. Bocheński, *La Logique de
Théophraste*, p. 39, translates λεκτόν as *le sens objectif*.
[63] Frege, *op. cit.*, p. 30.
[64] Ammonius, *In De Interp.*, ed. Busse, p. 17, line 27. Note that τὸ πρᾶγμα is used
here in the Peripatetic sense and not in that of the Stoics, according to which it would
be synonymous with τὸ λεκτόν.

nary) sense? To answer the question, we consider the four classes of expressions mentioned in rows *b* to *e* of table 1: individual names, class names, predicate expressions, and sentences.

According to the Stoic theory, the Lekton corresponding to an individual name[65] is a characteristic which is peculiar to an individual. Frege nowhere gives so explicit a statement of what he takes to be the sense of an individual name (*Eigenname*), but it seems more or less clear that he does not completely agree with the Stoics. Let us consider one of Frege's examples. For the individual name "Aristotle," he says, one might take as sense: the student of Plato and the teacher of Alexander the Great.[66] The Stoic Lekton for "Aristotle" would in this case be the property of being Plato's student and Alexander's teacher.[67]

Carnap takes what he calls "the individual concept" as the intension of an individual expression. He says, "It seems reasonable to assume that what he [Frege] means by the sense of an individual expression is about the same as what we mean by an individual concept."[68] Consequently, it appears that both Frege and Carnap differ from the Stoics on this point. But the Stoic proposal is at least as plausible as theirs. Frege and Carnap agree with the Stoics in regarding the intension of a class name as a property belonging to the individuals who are members of the class. What could be more natural than to identify individuals with their unit-classes and thus to consider an individual name as expressing a property that belongs only to one individual?[69]

With regard to the extension of an individual expression, we find no special term in Frege's theory or in that of the Stoics. Carnap uses the term "individual."[70] It is necessary here, however, to point out a certain superiority of the modern over the ancient view. The Stoics asserted flatly, in accordance with their materialism, that the objects denoted by all expressions are bodies, just as the signs are bodies. No such metaphysical opinion is mixed into the semantics of Frege or Carnap. To be sure, Frege takes up arms against the skeptics and idealists who say

---

[65] It was Chrysippus himself who split ὀνόματα into ὀνόματα proper and προσηγορίαι, according to Steinthal, *op. cit.*, p. 297.

[66] Frege, *op. cit.*, p. 27 n. Evidently the descriptive phrase here occurs in an oblique context.

[67] The Stoic treatment of proper names reminds one somewhat of W. V. Quine's procedure for the elimination of proper names; see his *Mathematical Logic* (New York, Norton, 1940), pp. 149 ff.

[68] Carnap, *op. cit.*, p. 126.

[69] Of interest in this connection is the Stoic definition of the individual as a species which contains no other species; correspondingly, the universal class was defined as the species which is contained in no other species. Diog. L., *Vitae* VII, 61.

[70] However, Frege's example, "Aristotle," and the Stoic example, "Dion," show that Frege and the Stoics would have agreed with Carnap in this matter. Thus the denotation of "Dion" is said to be Dion himself. Cf. Frege, *op. cit.*, p. 27 n.; Sextus, *Adv. Math.* VIII, 12.

that no expression has a denotation; he points out that we usually *intend* to talk about something more than our own ideas; that we usually *assume* that our expressions have denotations; and, further, that even if we are in error in this assumption, our intention is justification enough for introducing the concept of denotation.[71] But this plainly is not an argument against any metaphysical view. Carnap also makes no metaphysical assumption part of his definition or explication of "extension." It would seem, further, that the Stoics had need of some sort of theory of types or levels, else their view would have excluded propositions about propositions; but we have no clues to their treatment of this problem (if they ever thought of it).

Next, let us consider the terms occurring in row *c* of the table. Here we find that Carnap regards the intensions of class names as properties; indeed, he shows how classes themselves can be regarded as properties of a special kind.[72] The Stoics seem to agree with him in regard to the names. The Lekton of a class name ($\pi\rho\sigma\eta\gamma o\rho\iota\alpha$) is a property belonging to several individuals ($\dot{\eta}$ κοινὴ ποιότης). However, it must be confessed that the agreement may not be so striking as it seems. There is much doubt that the Stoics would have applied the term ποιότης wherever Carnap would use "property." The only examples of class names mentioned in the relevant Stoic fragments are "man," "horse," "goddess," and "wrath."[73] Each of these seems to be the name of a species;[74] possibly a ποιότης is the defining property of members of a genus or species, for example, "manhood." Its etymology faintly suggests this.[75] At any rate, it seems that the Stoics did not regard every collection of things as a genus or species,[76] although their definition of an individual as a species which contains no other species may cast some doubt here.[77]

Frege does not tell us what the denotation of a class name is, nor, for that matter, does he even use a specific term for class names. Church, carrying out what may be Frege's intentions, takes classes as denotations for predicate expressions; and it may be supposed that Frege would have assigned the same denotation to class names as to the corresponding predicate expressions.[78] If so, he would have agreed with Carnap. The Stoics are silent on this; we know only that the τυγχάνον for a class name

[71] Frege, *op. cit.*, pp. 31–32.
[72] Carnap, *op. cit.*, p. 93.
[73] Diog. L., *Vitae* VII, 58; Sextus, *Adv. Math.* I, 133.
[74] Cf. *Vitae* VII, 61.
[75] It means, etymologically, "the state of being-of-some-sort."
[76] *Vitae* VII, 60.
[77] *Ibid.*, 61.
[78] A. Church, review of Carnap's *Introduction to Semantics*, in *The Philosophical Review*, vol. 52 (1943), pp. 298–304 (cited in Carnap, *Meaning and Necessity*, p. 125).

will be corporeal, whatever it is. With respect to the sense of such terms, one may infer that Frege would have used the word *Subjekt* to cover the sense both of individual names and of predicate expressions. This would correspond exactly to the Stoic term πτῶσις, for, just as Frege says that every proposition (*Gedanke*) is composed of *Subjekt* and *Prädikat*,[79] so the Stoics said that a proposition (ἀξίωμα) is composed of πτῶσις and κατηγόρημα.[80]

The Stoic term ῥῆμα seems to correspond fairly closely to Carnap's term "predicate." Its Lekton is called a simple κατηγόρημα,[81] and again, just as an individual name or class name combines with a predicate expression to form a sentence, so a πτῶσις combines with a κατηγόρημα to form an ἀξίωμα. For this reason the terms "predicate" and "subject" have been chosen as translations for κατηγόρημα and πτῶσις, respectively. Again, Frege uses no term specifically for predicate expressions, but apparently he would apply the term *Prädikat* to their senses. According to Carnap, the intension of a predicator is a property—the same property that is the intension of the corresponding class name.

The question then arises: What is the Stoic distinction between ἡ ποιότης and τὸ κατηγόρημα, between the Lekton of a class name and that of a predicate expression? This is a question which the present writer does not know how to answer. Apparently the Stoics did not think that every true assertion about an entity expressed a ποιότης of that entity. It might instead express only a πως ἔχον of the entity, or a πρός τί πως ἔχον. But the predicate expression of any sentence does express a κατηγόρημα, according to them. Probably a more adequate account of the Stoic theory of categories would be required for answering the question adequately.

Proceeding to row *e*, we find that there is complete agreement about the intension of sentences: the Stoics, Frege, and Carnap all say that the intension of a sentence is a proposition.[82] But in the Stoic theory there is no trace of the Frege-Carnap notion that the extension of a sentence is its truth-value. Against the Epicureans, who maintained that "truth should be regarded as a predicate of certain sounds," the Stoics said

---

[79] Frege, *op. cit.*, p. 35.

[80] Diog. L., *Vitae* VII, 64: (Ἔστι δὲ τὸ κατηγόρημα . . . λεκτὸν ἐλλιπὲς συντακτὸν ὀρθῇ πτώσει πρὸς ἀξιώματος γένεσιν. Cf. Frege, *op. cit.*, p. 35: "Subjekt und Prädikat sind ja (im logischen Sinne verstanden) Gedankentheile." Cf. Carnap, *Meaning and Necessity*, p. 31: "By going one step further in the analysis of this proposition we find as its components the property Human and the individual concept Walter Scott; these components are both exemplified, and they are combined in a structure of propositional type."

[81] *Vitae* VII, 58.

[82] For λόγος ≡ *Satz*, see Steinthal, *op. cit.*, p. 292.

that truth is "about" (i.e., has to do with) the Lekton.[83] Elsewhere they described the relation as being such that truth is *in* the Lekton.[84] They nowhere suggested that the relation between the proposition and truth is in any way similar to that between, for example, the Lekton of an individual name and the externally existing individual. The Stoic notion of truth will be described more fully in the next chapter.

Concluding our comparison of the Stoic and modern semantical views, we may say that they are remarkably similar, especially in regard to the intension of the various linguistic expressions. This is shown by (1) the agreement among the three theories on the entities chosen as intensions for the various types of expressions, and (2) the fact that all three views assert that the intension of a part of a sentence is a part of the intension of the sentence. There are also certain similarities of general outlook. For instance, the Stoics were apparently quite as reluctant as Carnap to admit "metaphysical" entities like propositions; nevertheless, they did. However, it is quite possible that if more were known about the Stoic doctrine, many important disagreements with the modern analyses would become evident. Even a single Stoic εἰσαγωγή would enable us to give an immeasurably better account of Stoic views in logic and semantics. One need only imagine someone in A.D. 4,000 studying Frege's theories by the sole means of a few hostile reviews in some nontechnical periodical in order to appreciate the fact that the scraps of Stoic doctrine are as clear and consistent as they are.

---

[83] Sextus, *Adv. Math.* VIII, 11–13.
[84] *Ibid.*, 70.

CHAPTER III

PROPOSITIONS, TRUTH, AND NECESSITY

SUMMARY

THIS CHAPTER is divided into three sections. The first defines and classi-
fies propositions and discusses their fundamental properties. A proposition is said to be "a complete Lekton assertoric in itself." Its most basic
property is that of being true or false and not both. Propositions are
classified as atomic and molecular; each of these classes in turn is divided
into several subclasses. The absence from Stoic logic of examples beginning with "all" is noted. In the second section, the many Stoic usages of
the words "truth" and "true" are taken up seriatim. All these usages are
definable in terms of the usage referring to propositions. The third section deals with Stoic notions of necessity and possibility, as found in the
fragments of certain (Megarian) philosophers to whom the notions were
originally due. It is shown that a reference to time plays a very important
role in Diodorus' view of possibility. (This is closely connected with his
position in the controversy over implication, to be discussed in chap. iv.)
A brief account of what is known of the famous "Master" argument of
Diodorus is included, together with a few remarks on the views of Philo
and Chrysippus regarding possibility.

§ 1: PROPOSITIONS

Aulus Gellius[1] relates that after his return to Rome from Athens he
decided to take a short course in logic. Accordingly he procured a Stoic
textbook—a Greek introduction to logic (εἰσαγωγὴ διαλεκτική)[2]—and applied himself to it. The first chapter was entitled "On Propositions" (περὶ
ἀξιωμάτων).[3] Apparently Gellius found it quite difficult, for he began to
search diligently for a Latin commentary. He finally discovered one in
the library and read it carefully. Unfortunately, it contained nothing
that clarified matters; on the contrary, he reports, its author (Lucius
Aelius) had written the book against his own forgetfulness rather than
for the instruction of others.

Of necessity, therefore, Gellius returned to his Greek book. In it he
found the Stoic definition of proposition: "a complete Lekton, assertoric

---

[1] *Noctes Atticae* XVI, viii.

[2] This was the standard title for Stoic introductions to logic. It is also the title of
the extant treatise by Galen. See chap. i, § 3.

[3] This too, was a standard title, referred to by Sextus, Diogenes, Boethius, Proclus,
and others.

by itself."[4] There were also some examples: "Hannibal was a Carthaginian," "Scipio destroyed Numantia," "Milo was convicted of murder,"
"Pleasure is neither good nor evil." In fact, says Gellius, any full and
complete thought that is so expressed in words that it is necessarily
either true or false is called "proposition" (ἀξίωμα) by the logicians.
Gellius says further that Varro, who was the author of *De Lingua Latina*,
used the term *proloquium*, and that Cicero[5] said that he would use the
term *pronuntiatum* until he could find a better one. (We know that
Cicero did find a better one—*enuntiatio*.[6]) Gellius then goes on to discuss
conditionals, conjunctions, disjunctions, and other types of molecular
propositions. These will be considered later.

The report of Gellius is in complete agreement with our other sources.
His definition of "proposition" is:

$$\text{λεκτὸν αὐτοτελὲς ἀπόφαντον ὅσον ἔφ' αὐτῷ}$$

The version given by Sextus[7] is:

$$\text{λεκτὸν αὐτοτελὲς ἀπόφαντον ὅσον ἔφ' ἑαυτῷ}$$

And Diogenes[8] gives the following:

$$\text{πρᾶγμα αὐτοτελὲς ἀπόφαντον ὅσον ἔφ' ἑαυτῷ}$$

(It is to be observed that in such contexts as these the term πρᾶγμα has
the same denotation as λεκτόν.) There are numerous other clear references
to this definition; undoubtedly it was to be found in almost every Stoic
introduction.

Every proposition, according to the Stoics, is true or false. Possibly,
for some members of the school, this was a matter of definition. Thus
both Sextus and Diogenes quote the same statement: ἀξίωμα δέ ἐστιν ὅ
ἐστιν ἀληθὲς ἢ ψεῦδος, though neither calls it a definition.[9] We do know,

---

[4] Rolfe's translation (Loeb ed., vol. 3, p. 158, note 4), "an absolute and self-evident
proposition," misses the mark completely. ἀξίωμα did not mean "axiom" in Stoic logic,
despite Ammonius, *In An. Pr.*, ed. Wallies, p. 26, line 36.

[5] *Tusc. Disp.* I, 7, 14.

[6] *De Fato*, 1. Apuleius, *In De Interp.*, ed. Oud., 265, says that Cicero used *enuntia-
tum*. Apuleius also agrees with Gellius that a proposition expresses a complete
thought (*absoluta sententia*).

[7] *Hyp. Pyrrh.* II, 104.

[8] *Vitae* VII, 65. Hicks' translation, "a thing complete in itself, capable of being
denied [*sic*] in and by itself," is inadequate. πρᾶγμα here means the same as λεκτόν
(see Glossary), as is very plain in the section preceding the one cited; and ἀπόφαντος
comes from ἀποφαίνω, not from ἀποφάσκω or ἀπόφημι.

[9] Sextus, *Adv. Math.* VIII, 12; Diog. L., *Vitae* VII, 65, 66. Cf. Simplicius, *In Cat.*,
ed. Kalbfleisch, p. 406, line 22; Cicero, *Tusc. Disp.* I, 7, 14, *De Fato*, 20, 38. But Cicero,
Acad. II, 95, *does* call it a definition (and a "fundament of dialectic"). Simplicius
(*SVF* II, 198) shows how it can be proved that any proposition is either true or false:

however, that the Stoics regarded it as an assertion against Aristotle[10] and the Epicureans,[11] whom they believed to have held that propositions about future contingencies were neither true nor false. Apparently it was Chrysippus who defended the *tertium non datur* most vigorously. In at least three places in *De Fato*[12] Cicero ascribes the view to Chrysippus; in one place[13] he says that Chrysippus tried *omnis nervos* to persuade people of this fact. There is no doubt that nearly all the Stoics shared the same view. Sometimes it was stated as "Every proposition is true or false"; sometimes as "The disjunction [διεξευγμένον] of a proposition with its negation is necessarily true."[14] Since the Stoics always used διεξευγμένον for exclusive disjunction, there seems to be no point in trying (with Łukasiewicz) to find a distinction here between the law of contradiction and the law of excluded middle.[15]

The Stoics divide propositions into those that are atomic and those that are molecular.[16] They take care to point out, however, that atomic propositions are not called "atomic" because they have no parts; it is rather because their parts are not occurrences of propositions.[17] An atomic proposition is one which is constructed of subject (πτῶσις) and predicate (κατηγόρημα) without the help of a logical connective (σύνδεσμος). A molecular proposition consists either of two occurrences of a single proposition or of different propositions, and is always recognizable by the presence in it of one or more logical connectives. The provision in this definition for two occurrences of the same proposition may show that the distinction between propositions and sentences was not forgotten.

"If there will be a naval battle tomorrow, it is true to say that there will be; if there will not, it is false to say that there will be. Either there will be a battle or there will not be. Therefore, either it is true or false to say that there will be."

[10] Boethius, *In De Interp.*, ed. secunda, Meiser, 208. This refers to chap. 9 of *De Interpretatione*.

[11] Cicero, *De Fato*, 37.

[12] *Ibid.*, 37, 20–21.

[13] *Ibid.*, 21.

[14] See Cicero, *Acad. II*, 97.

[15] Łukasiewicz, "Philosophische Bemerkungen . . . ," pp. 63 ff. I do not deny that the Stoics had a notion of inclusive disjunction (παραδιεξευγμένον), but this connective does not occur in their five basic undemonstrated argument schemata.

[16] Sextus, *Adv. Math.* VIII, 93; Diog. L., *Vitae* VII, 68; Galen, *Inst. Log.*, 12; *SVF* II, 182. The classification of propositions is schematized in figure 2, p. 16. Cf. the Peripatetic distinction, Apuleius, *In De Interp.*, ed. Oud., 266. It does not seem that the Stoics were careful in their definition of σύνδεσμος, for a connective is defined as a sign, and yet it joins the parts of a proposition.

[17] Sextus, *Adv. Math.* VIII, 94. The parts of a proposition are the Lekta corresponding to individual or class names (ὀνόματα or προσηγορίαι) and predicate expressions (ῥήματα). Thus we find Sextus objecting that only corporeal things can be divided and that therefore propositions cannot be compounds (VIII, 79). Whether the premise of this argument was taken from Stoic physics is unknown.

Several kinds of atomic propositions are listed by the Stoics. Sextus mentions three: definite, indefinite, and intermediate.[18] Definite propositions are asserted deictically: "This [man] is walking," "This [man] is sitting," with the speaker indicating the person concerned. Indefinite propositions lie in the scope of ("are governed by") an indefinite particle; for instance, "Somebody is walking." Intermediate propositions are neither indefinite, since they refer to a particular object, nor definite, since they are not uttered deictically; for example, "Socrates is walking" or "Socrates is sitting." Definite and indefinite propositions are related, according to the Stoics, as follows: the indefinite proposition cannot be true unless the corresponding definite proposition is true. For example, unless "This person is walking" is true of some particular person, the proposition "Somebody is walking" is not true.[19] Similarly, intermediate and definite propositions are said to be related in such a way that if an intermediate proposition is true, then for some particular person the corresponding definite proposition is true (with certain exceptions, as will now be shown).[20]

The latter point is brought out by Chrysippus in a paradox which he offered against the Peripatetics.[21] On the one hand, he argues that an intermediate proposition can be true only if there is some particular person with reference to whom the corresponding definite proposition is true. For instance (not his example), if "Dion is at Athens" is true, then, with some appropriate indication, "This man is at Athens" must be true. On the other hand, however, he argued that in the intermediate proposition, "Dion has died," there is no possible indication such that "This man has died" is true.[22] It is easy to see that the solution of this paradox would be accomplished by means of the Stoic distinction between the Lekton of a sign and the external object corresponding to it.

Diogenes, too, lists definite, indefinite, and intermediate propositions as types of atomic proposition.[23] According to his version, the definite proposition is one composed of the Lekton of an indicative sign, plus a

---

[18] *Adv. Math.* VIII, 96, 100. Note that what the Peripatetics called "indefinite" propositions (e.g., "An animal is breathing") would be "intermediate" propositions according to the Stoics. Cf. Apuleius, *In De Interp.*, ed. Oud., 266.

[19] *Adv. Math.* VIII, 98.

[20] See Alexander, *In An. Pr.*, ed. Wallies, 177–178. Cf. Ammonius, *In An. Pr.*, ed. Wallies, p. 50, line 13.

[21] Alexander, *In An. Pr.*, 177–178. This argument was put forward specifically as a challenge to the Diodorean proposition that an impossible proposition could not logically follow from a possible proposition.

[22] Philoponus, *In An. Pr.*, ed. Wallies, p. 166, lines 3 ff., explains this as follows: "The word τοῦτο, being deictic, signifies something which exists, but the word τεθνάναι signifies something that does not exist. It is impossible for that which exists not to exist. Therefore, that this man has died [τοῦτο τεθνάναι] is impossible."

[23] Diog. L., *Vitae* VII, 69.

predicate; the indefinite is composed of one or more indefinite particles, plus a predicate; and the intermediate, which Diogenes calls the "categorical," is composed of a predicate and a subject in the nominative case. He also lists some further types of atomic proposition, namely, denials, privations, and negations.

A denial (ἀρνητικόν) is an atomic proposition composed of a denying particle and a predicate.[24] For example, in "No-one is walking" (οὐδεὶς περιπατεῖ), "No-one" (οὐδείς) is the denying particle (μόριον ἀρνητικόν) and "is walking" is the predicate (κατηγόρημα). A privation is an atomic proposition formed from another atomic proposition by reversing the predicate: "This man is unkind."[25]

A negation (ἀποφατικόν), to be sharply distinguished from a denial (ἀρνητικόν), is formed from a proposition by prefixing the negative "not" (οὐκ).[26] The account of Diogenes seems to suggest that negations are atomic propositions; the account of Sextus does not substantiate this. Among the Stoic fragments are many examples of propositions which are negations and which nevertheless contain connectives. In fact, the Stoics made a great point of the observation that in order properly to negate a proposition one must *prefix* the negation sign. Thus, they said, "It is day and it is not night" is not the negation of "It is day and it is night"; but the correct negation is "Not both: it is day and it is night."[27] It is an interesting fact that, in this particular, the Greek language is superior to English, for the Greek negative may be placed at the beginning of the sentence—οὐχὶ ἡμέρα ἐστίν; in English this would be solecistic—"Not: it is day." According to one source,[28] the Stoics used the term "negation" *only* for propositions that were preceded by the negative. A double negation (ὑπεραποφατικόν) is the negation of a negation: "Not: it is not day." It "posits" (τίθησι) the corresponding unnegated proposition, "It is day." Unfortunately, the example of a double negation given by Diogenes, οὐχὶ ἡμέρα οὐκ ἔστιν, is difficult to reconcile with the preceding rule about prefixing the negative particle.[29]

---

[24] *Ibid.*, 70.
[25] *Ibid.*
[26] *Ibid.*, 69. Cf. the Glossary, s.v. ἀντικείμενον and ἀποφατικόν. Sextus, *Adv. Math.* VIII, 89–90; Apuleius, *In De Interp.*, ed. Oud., 266; Boethius, *In De Interp.*, ed. secunda, Meiser, 261; Apollonius of Alexandria, Περὶ Συνδέσμων, ed. Schneider, 218.
[27] See Sextus, *Adv. Math.* VIII, 89 ff. Note the explanation in terms of the scope of the negative. The scope of "not" in a negated conjunction may be the point of the paradox offered by Sextus at *Hyp. Pyrrh.* II, 241, but I would be inclined to adopt Weber's emendation of the text (see the *apparatus criticus* of Mutschmann's edition).
[28] Apuleius, *In De Interp.*, 266.
[29] Diog. L., *Vitae* VII, 69. Prantl, by confusing the complement of a class with the negation of a proposition, makes dreadful mistakes (*Geschichte der Logik im Abendlande*, vol. 1, pp. 449–450). He did not, however, generate this confusion by himself;

It will be noticed that nowhere in the rather elaborate classification is any provision made for universal affirmative propositions, that is, for propositions beginning with "all.", This may be a mere coincidence. However, it will be observed also that, of the many propositions mentioned by the Stoics as examples for illustrating the various parts of their logic, not a single one begins with "all." The reason for this may be connected in some way with the alleged nominalism of the Stoics;[30] or possibly the Stoics interpreted what we would consider universal propositions as propositions about the corresponding class; or, again, perhaps they regarded these simply as equivalent to the negations of indefinite propositions. At any rate, the present writer is unable to offer any evidenced explanation.[31]

So much for the Stoic account of atomic propositions. There would be much more to say about them if the Stoic works were extant, for Chrysippus alone wrote at least one book on each kind of atomic proposition and three on negation.[32]

A molecular proposition is always marked by the occurrence of a connective ($\sigma\acute{v}\nu\delta\epsilon\sigma\mu o\varsigma$) or connectives in the corresponding sentence. A connective is an indeclinable part of speech which joins the parts of the sentence.[33] Molecular propositions, accordingly, are classified on the basis of the connectives they contain (at the main break).[34] Thus there is the

---

rather, he borrowed it from the Aristotelian commentators, Simplicius and Boethius. The latter were trying to subsume the theory of the hypothetical syllogism under that of the categorical syllogism, and in their attempts regularly confounded propositional variables with class variables. In the relatively good sources of Stoic doctrine, however—Sextus, Diogenes, and Galen—one does not find this confusion; in fact, one finds no established way of forming an expression for the complement of a class.

It is interesting to observe that the Stoics had no need of a rule for double negation. By means of a type 4 undemonstrated argument and the law of excluded middle, one could always pass from a proposition to its double negation; similarly, by means of a type 5 undemonstrated argument, one could return. Thus:

> Either it is day or it is not day.
> It is day.
> Therefore, not: it is not day.

> Either it is day or it is not day.
> Not: it is not day.
> Therefore, it is day.

"Or" is here used in its exclusive sense, of course.

[30] On Stoic and Cynic nominalism see Zeller, *op. cit.*, vol. 2, part 1, pp. 295 ff., and vol. 3, part 1, p. 80.

[31] Sextus tells us that the definition "Man is a mortal rational animal" has the same meaning as "If x is a man, then x is a mortal rational animal," and he calls the latter $\kappa\alpha\theta o\lambda\iota\kappa\acute{o}v$. Chrysippus is mentioned, but one cannot tell whether the term was his or Sextus'. Sextus, *Adv. Math.* XI, 8.

[32] Diog. L., *Vitae* VII, 190.

[33] *Ibid.*, 58.

[34] *Ibid.*, 71 ff.; cf. *SVF* II, 182.

conditional (συνημμένον), the conjunction (συμπεπλεγμένον) the disjunction (διεζευγμένον), and several others. A conditional proposition is one that is formed from two occurrences of a single proposition or from different propositions by means of the connective "if" (εἰ or εἴπερ). It asserts that the part which does not immediately follow the "if" is a consequence of the part which does immediately follow the "if."[35] The conditions for its truth were the subject of great debate among the Stoics and will be discussed in the next chapter. A conjunction is a molecular proposition compounded by means of the connective "and" (καί): "It is day and it is light." A disjunction is put together by means of the connective "or" (ἤ), which is always to be understood in an exclusive sense. The disjunction asserts that the disjuncts are not both true nor both false. Thus, a favorite Stoic example is, "It is day or it is night." There are further the so-called "quasi-disjunction" (ὁμοιῶς διεζευγμένον) and "pseudo-disjunction" (παραδιεζευγμένον); the latter corresponds to our "inclusive disjunction." These, together with the quasi- and pseudo-conditionals, will be defined and discussed in the next chapter.

In addition to the foregoing, Diogenes lists certain non-truth-functional types of molecular proposition.[36] The causal proposition is constructed by means of the connective "because." For example, "Because it is day, it is light." In these, "The antecedent is *as it were* [οἱονεί] a cause of the consequent." There are also certain molecular propositions of this sort: "More likely it is day than it is night." These are called "propositions indicating greater probability" and are formed by placing the connective "more likely" in front of the first component and the connective "than" in between the two components. In a corresponding way, the so-called "propositions indicating less probability" are formed: "Less likely it is day than it is night."

§ 2: Truth

The student of Stoic logic finds that it is relatively clear and unambiguous on most of the important points, but the discussion of truth is a notable exception. Nevertheless, since the notion of truth plays a fundamental role in logic, and since we are striving to give a complete account of what is known of Stoic logic, we must include an exposition of the views of Stoics on this subject.

The Stoics appear to have used the word "true" in many different senses. First and foremost, they spoke of truth as being "in" or "about"

---

[35] Cf. *Adv. Math.* VIII, 111.
[36] *Vitae* VII, 72 ff.

propositions.[37] This seems to be the basic usage of the word in Stoic logic. Closely connected with this is the sense in which certain propositional functions are said to be true for all or some values of their variables.[38] Next, it was applied to the so-called "presentations" ($\phi\alpha\nu$-$\tau\alpha\sigma\iota\alpha\iota$).[39] A presentation is true if and only if a proposition accurately describing it is true. Suppose that, judging by my present $\phi\alpha\nu\tau\alpha\sigma\iota\alpha$, I say, "It is day." If it is in fact day, then the proposition is true, and so is the presentation. A false presentation is such that a proposition adequately describing it will be false. So, for example, when I see an oar that is partially under water, I may describe my presentation accurately and say, "The oar is bent," but since the oar is not bent, the proposition and the presentation are false.

The classes of true and false presentations are neither mutually exclusive nor mutually exhaustive; some presentations are both true and false, and some are neither. For an example of a presentation that is both true and false, Sextus cites the image of Electra visualized by Orestes in his madness. Sextus explains that this presentation was true so far as it was caused by something that existed, since Electra existed, but that it was false so far as it seemed to be a presentation of a Fury, since actually there was no Fury. The examples given, unfortunately, do not differentiate clearly between false presentations and those that are both true and false. For there seems to be as much reason for saying that the presentation of the bent oar was true so far as it came from an existing object as there is reason for regarding Orestes' vision of Electra as true in one respect. Prospects of clearing up this confusion are slight, since the issue is not discussed in any other fragment, and the remaining examples given here are equally indecisive.[40] The notion of presentations that are neither true nor false is still more cryptic: "The presentations that are neither true nor false are the *generic* presentations; for the *genera* of things of which the species are of this kind or of that kind are not of this kind or of that kind.[41] For example, some men are Greeks and some men are barbarians, but the generic Man is neither Greek (for then all men would have been of the species Greek) nor barbarian (for the

---

[37] *Adv. Math.* VIII, 11, 70.

[38] Thus, expressions like "It is day" are said to "become true" or "become false." See the discussion of Diodorean sentences in the next section of the text.

[39] *Adv. Math.* VII, 243 ff.

[40] Another example of a false presentation is, "The Porch is tapering." For the meaning cf. *Hyp. Pyrrh.* I, 118. Another example of a presentation that is both true and false is, "when a man imagines in his dreams that Dion is standing beside him (when Dion is alive)."

[41] Note that this sort of statement, which men for two thousand years have thought to be true and worth saying, is nonsensical according to the theory of types, and so is the reason given for it in the example.

same reason)." Correct interpretation of this passage awaits further
investigation. In still a fourth sense, "true" was applied by the Stoics
to arguments. This will be discussed more fully in chapter iv, and we
include only a definition here: an argument is true if and only if it is
valid and has true premises. If it is invalid or has a false premise, then
it is said to be false.[42]

Thus there are at least four senses of "true." Now it might be thought
that "truth" meant merely the characteristic of being true and that
consequently when the senses of "true" were determined, the senses of
"truth" would *ipso facto* be determined. In Stoic usage, this was not
the case.

Sextus describes, in two long passages which corroborate one another
in every detail, a Stoic distinction between the true (τὸ ἀληθές) and truth
(ἡ ἀλήθεια).[43] The Stoics say, according to him, that the true differs from
truth in three ways: in essence, in constitution, and in meaning. They
differ in essence because the true is incorporeal (for it is a proposition,
and a proposition is a Lekton, and a Lekton is incorporeal), whereas
truth is a body. For truth is knowledge assertoric of all true propositions,
and knowledge is the principal part of the soul in a certain state (πως
ἔχον, the third Stoic category). The soul, in turn, was regarded by the
Stoics as a body (the breath). Thus, just as a fist is a body because it is
only a hand in a certain state, so knowledge is a body, since it is only
the principal part of the soul in a certain state.

Truth and the true differ in constitution, since truth involves knowledge of many truths, while the true is something simple; for example, "I
am conversing" (this in spite of the fact that the proposition is described
in many places as a σύνθετον).[44] They differ also in meaning (δυνάμει),
since truth pertains to knowledge, while the true does not; also, truth
is found only in a good man, but even a bad man may say something
true. In connection with the latter point, the Stoics distinguished between lying and telling falsehoods. The good man may tell a falsehood,
perhaps because of his urbanity or perhaps because he is a physician or
an army officer; but the good man cannot be a liar. It is not the act itself
but the motive that counts; for example, says Sextus, grave-digging
may be an honorable or a base profession depending on the reasons why
the graves are dug.

The criterion for determining the truth of presentations, much discussed by the Stoics, is an epistemological problem and not within the

---

[42] *Hyp. Pyrrh.* II, 138 ff.
[43] *Ibid.*, 81 ff.; *Adv. Math.* VII, 38 ff.
[44] *Adv. Math.* VIII, 79.

scope of this work. Propositions are said to be true when the thing named
by the subject name has the predicate expressed by the predicate expression. Thus, "This man is sitting" is true when the object indicated has
the predicate in question, "is sitting."[45] Diogenes, using a different
example, tells us that "It is day" is true if it is day; if it is not day, the
proposition is false.[46] Other passages express the same notion.[47]

§ 3: NECESSITY AND POSSIBILITY

Mention has previously been made of the fact that arguments went on
within the Stoic school over the interpretation of conditionals. The origi-
nators of the three dominant views were Diodorus Cronus, Philo, and
Chrysippus. These men also had theories about the proper definitions
of "necessity" and "possibility," and it will be seen in the sequel that
their theories of the conditional were very closely connected with their
theories about necessity. Accordingly, it seems desirable to give a brief
account of the Stoic views on necessity and possibility.

The task of understanding the theory of Diodorus Cronus[48] is made
difficult by the fact that he apparently thought of propositions as though
they contained time-variables. His examples always include expressions
like "It is day," and he says that these are true at certain times and false
at others, or that they become true and become false. It seems, therefore,
that instead of dealing with what would today be called "propositions,"
he in effect considered the corresponding functions formed by adding
"at t" to each proposition: "Snow is white at t," "Grass is green at t,"
"It is day at t," etc. Thus "(t) (Snow is white at t)" would represent the
Diodorean-type proposition " 'Snow is white' is always [ἀεί] true"; and
"(Et) (Snow is white at t)" would represent the statement " 'Snow is
white' is sometimes [ποτέ] true." (Here the words "always" and "sometimes" are of course to be taken in a temporal sense.) If we further sym-
bolize the present moment by t' and the relation of temporal precedence
by $<$, we can express such Diodorean statements as " 'It is night' will
be true" and " 'It is night' will never again be true." These become,
respectively,

$$(Et)\ (t' < t\ .\ \text{It is night at } t)$$

and

$$\sim(Et)\ (t' < t\ .\ \text{It is night at } t).$$

Now the famous Diodorean definition of "possible," which was known
throughout antiquity and was the subject of whole books of criticism, is

---

[45] *Ibid.*, 100.
[46] *Vitae* VII, 65.
[47] *SVF* II, 198.
[48] Much of the following description of Diodorus' theory is included in my article,
"Diodorean Implication."

usually given as follows: "The possible is that which either is or will be."[49]
This definition is mentioned by many ancient authors in many places;
but only Boethius gives Diodorus' definitions of the closely associated
terms "impossible," "necessary," "nonnecessary,"[50] which in turn show
clearly that the definition of "possible" was slightly elliptical; it should
have been, "The possible is that which either is or will be *true.*" The other
three definitions are as follows: "The impossible is that which, being false,
will not be true"; "The necessary is that which, being true, will not be false";
and "The nonnecessary is that which either is or will be false." Formali-
zation of these by the method mentioned above makes it clear that certain important requirements are satisfied:

(1) $\ulcorner p$ is possible at $t'\urcorner$ *for* $\ulcorner(p$ at $t') \lor (Et) (t' < t . p$ at $t)\urcorner$
(2) $\ulcorner p$ is impossible at $t'\urcorner$ *for* $\ulcorner\sim(p$ at $t') . (t) (t' < t \supset \sim(p$ at $t))\urcorner$
(3) $\ulcorner p$ is necessary at $t'\urcorner$ *for* $\ulcorner(p$ at $t') . (t) (t' < t \supset p$ at $t)\urcorner$
(4) $\ulcorner p$ is nonnecessary at $t'\urcorner$ *for* $\ulcorner\sim(p$ at $t') \lor (Et) (t' < t . \sim(p$ at $t)\urcorner$

Thus the definiens of (1) is the contradictory of the definiens of (2), as
it should be. Similarly the definiens of (3) is the contradictory of that of
(4). Further, it is evident that according to these definitions a proposition
is possible if and only if its negation is nonnecessary, and it is impossible
if and only if its negation is necessary.[51] Thus, whatever the other merits
of these definitions may be, one must admit that they bear the proper
relationships to one another.[52]

[49] Alexander, *In An. Pr.*, ed. Wallies, 184. Alexander gives some examples: "According to him (Diodorus) it is possible for me to be at Corinth if I am at Corinth or if I
am going to be at Corinth. But if I should never be at Corinth, it wouldn't have been
possible. And a child's becoming a grammarian is possible, if he ever does become one."

[50] Boethius, *In De Interp.*, ed. secunda, Meiser, 234.

[51] Assuming, in line with our interpretation of Diodorean statements, that $\ulcorner\sim(p$
at $t)\urcorner$ is equivalent to $\ulcorner(\sim p)$ at $t\urcorner$.

[52] It is interesting to note that Boethius himself did not understand the Stoic
definitions which he has preserved for us. He describes a Stoic division of propositions
as follows (p. 393): "They [the Stoics] divide propositions in this way: some propositions, they say, are possible, and others are impossible; and of the possible, some are
necessary and some are not necessary; and again of the nonnecessary, some are possible and others are impossible—by so doing they foolishly and recklessly set up the
possible as both genus and species of the nonnecessary." Doubtless Boethius is
thinking of this sort of diagram:

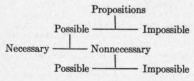

But no such diagram is implied by what he represents the Stoics as saying. Prantl,
op. cit., p. 463, makes the same error as Boethius. Cf. Zeller, *op. cit.*, vol. 3, part 1, p.
110, note 2.

Diodorus, apparently perceiving that all four definitions may be considered as depending upon the first one, attempted to construct an argument to justify it.[53] The resulting trilemma was called "the Master" (ὁ κυριεύων), and the great fame of Diodorus as a logician rested primarily upon it. But unfortunately we possess only enough information about the argument to make its actual nature a tantalizing problem. Several authors mention it by name, but it is discussed only by Epictetus,[54] and his account is too sketchy to be of much help. However, he did include this much: Diodorus argued that the following three propositions could not all be true.

(1) Every proposition true about the past is necessary.
(2) An impossible proposition may not follow from a possible one.
(3) There is a proposition which is possible, but which neither is true nor will be true.

Since, according to Epictetus, the first two propositions seemed to Diodorus to be more plausible than the third, he dropped the third, and this accounts for his definition of the possible as "that which either is true or will be true." Epictetus goes on to say that other philosophers chose different ways out of the difficulty. Cleanthes and his school accepted the second and third propositions while rejecting the first; Chrysippus accepted the first and third while denying the second. It is noteworthy that no one challenged Diodorus' argument that the three propositions were incompatible.

The question is, Why are they incompatible? There is hardly enough evidence to justify even a guess, but this, of course, has not prevented scholars from being certain about the matter. Zeller[55] thinks that Diodo-

---

[53] Alexander, *In An. Pr.*, ed. Wallies, p. 184. See note 49; the next sentence is, "And for the establishment of this [notion of possibility], the 'Master' argument was put forth by Diodorus."

[54] *Diss.* II, 19,1: ὁ κυριεύων λόγος ἀπὸ τοιούτων τινῶν ἀφορμῶν ἠρωτῆσθαι φαίνεται. Κοινῆς γὰρ οὔσης μάχης τοῖς τρισὶ τούτοις πρὸς ἄλληλα, τῷ Πᾶν παρεληλυθὸς ἀληθὲς ἀναγκαῖον εἶναι, καὶ τῷ Δυνατῷ ἀδύνατον μὴ ἀκολουθεῖν, καὶ τῷ Δύνατον εἶναι ὃ οὔτ' ἔστιν ἀληθὲς οὔτ' ἔσται. συνιδὼν τὴν μάχην ταύτην ὁ Διόδωρος τῇ τῶν πρώτων δυοῖν πιθανότητι συνεχρήσατο πρὸς παράστασιν τοῦ Μηδὲν εἶναι δυνατὸν ὃ οὔτ' ἔστιν ἀληθὲς οὔτ' ἔσται.

[55] Zeller, *op. cit.*, vol. 2, part 1, pp. 269-270. Cf. also Zeller's article, "Ueber den κυριεύων des Megarikers Diodorus," pp. 151-159, in which he states the argument as follows: " 'Wenn etwas möglich wäre, was weder ist noch sein wird, so würde aus einem Möglichen ein Unmögliches folgen; nun kann aber aus einem Möglichen kein Unmögliches folgen; also ist nichts möglich, was weder ist noch sein wird.' Der Untersatz dieses Schlusses, dass aus einem Möglichen kein Unmögliches folge, wurde als anerkannt vorausgesetzt. Der hypothetische Obersatz dagegen bedurfte einer weiteren Begründung, und er erhielt diese mittelst des Satzes, dass alles Vergangene nothwendig sei. Wenn nämlich von zwei sich gegenseitig ausschliessenden Fällen der eine eintritt, so ist ebendamit die Möglichkeit des andern aufgehoben, denn was einmal geschehen ist, lässt sich nicht ändern [πᾶν παρεληλυθὸς ἀναγκαῖον], dieser zweite Fall ist mithin jetzt unmöglich; wäre er daher früher möglich gewesen, so wäre, wie Diodor glaubt, aus einem Möglichen ein Unmögliches hervorgegangen." Compare also Prantl, *op. cit.*, pp. 40 ff.

rus, in the second proposition, was confusing logical with temporal consequence and that his argument was something like this. Suppose (in accordance with 3) that there is a proposition which is possible but which neither is at present true nor will be true. Then its negation is presently true and will always be true. As soon as the present becomes past, the negation of the proposition will become necessary (according to the first of Diodorus' propositions). But if its negation becomes necessary, the proposition itself becomes impossible. Thus a proposition which was possible will have become impossible, in violation of the second of Diodorus' propositions.

This explanation is not very satisfying. It rests, in the first place, on the notion that Diodorus confused temporal succession with logical consequence. But this hardly seems likely, for Diodorus himself was in the center of a very sophisticated debate over the nature of logical consequence. The word used in Epictetus' account is ἀκολουθεῖν, which is the same word used by Diodorus for "is a consequent of" in this debate. Further, it seems unlikely that Chrysippus would have overlooked so elementary a confusion; indeed, he objected to Diodorus' second proposition, but not on the grounds that it did not refer to logical consequence.[56]

But although it is easy to find objections to Zeller's explanation, it is not so easy to find a better one. Any good explanation should be compatible with the assumption that when Diodorus said δυνατῷ ἀδύνατον μὴ ἀκολουθεῖν he was using the word ἀκολουθεῖν in its Diodorean sense. But until further evidence is forthcoming, the possibility of finding a satisfactory explanation is almost eliminated by the fact that, although Diodorus usually predicates necessity of what are in effect propositional functions, it seems that in the first of his three incompatibles, necessity is predicated of a proposition. Consider the function "Socrates dies at t." Now this propositional function is satisfied for $t = 399$ B.C., but the function is certainly not necessary in the Diodorean sense, since it does not hold for all values of the time-variable. It presumably is the *proposition* "Socrates died in 399 B.C." that is now necessary.[57] Thus, in the first of

---

[56] Chrysippus challenged Diodorus' second proposition by trying to find a contrary instance. See note 21. Cf. also Plutarch, *De Stoic. Repugn.*, chap. 46, p. 1055d; Proclus, *In Plat. Parm.* IV, 103 (*SVF* II, 202b).

[57] Of course it is not entirely clear how Diodorus' first proposition is to be interpreted. I have supposed that it means the same as the scholastic principle cited by Leibniz in the "Theodicy" (*Phil. Schriften*, ed. Gerhardt, vol. 6, p. 131): "Unumquodque, quando est, oportet esse"—i.e., assuming a proposition to be true, it is necessary (since its negation implies a contradiction). Cf. Aristotle, *De Interp.*, 9, 19a23: τὸ μὲν οὖν εἶναι τὸ ὂν ὅταν ᾖ, καὶ τὸ μὴ ὂν μὴ εἶναι, ὅταν μὴ ᾖ, ἀνάγκη. οὐ μὴν οὔτε τὸ ὂν ἅπαν ἀνάγκη εἶναι οὔτε τὸ μὴ ὂν μὴ εἶναι.

Diodorus' incompatible propositions, the word "necessary" seems to be used in a sense different from that in which he ordinarily used it.

For Philo's views on possibility the best source again is Boethius' commentary.[58] There we learn that, according to Philo, a proposition is possible "if in its internal nature it is susceptible of truth." Thus the proposition "Today I am going to read Theocritus' *Bucolics* again" is said to be possible according to Philo's criterion, since (as far as its nature is concerned) it can be asserted truly if nothing external prevents the occurrence. "The necessary" is defined as "that which, being true, is in its very nature not susceptible of falsehood." "The nonnecessary" is "that which in its nature is susceptible of falsehood." Correspondingly, "the impossible" is "that which according to its nature is not susceptible of truth."

The other sources are in general agreement with this account of Philo's view. Thus Simplicius, discussing how one is to decide whether something is knowable or perceptible, says, "Shall we decide by the 'fitness' [ἐπιτηδειότητα] alone, as Philo said, even if there is no knowledge of it nor ever will be?" By way of example, he says that a piece of wood in the Atlantic Ocean is combustible "in itself and according to its own nature," though probably it will never be burned.[59] Alexander mentions the same example in his account, and says that Philo judged possibility by "the mere 'fitness' [ἐπιτηδειότητα] of existing even if it should be prevented from existing by external necessity."[60] The last remark, about external necessity, may seem puzzling.[61] Philoponus' account shows the circularity of Philo's definition most clearly: "Philo says the possible is that which either has occurred or that which may possibly occur but never does occur."[62] Philoponus' example is that a shell at the bottom of the sea is perceptible, even if no one will ever see it. His version, like Alexander's, does not quite jibe with what Boethius reported; but apparently the essential point is that Philo judged the possibility of an event by reference to its internal fitness to occur and not by reference to whether or not it will occur.

Little is known of Chrysippus' view except that, in disagreement with Diodorus, he maintained that certain events which will never take place are none the less possible.[63] Also, he claimed that it was not necessary

[58] Boethius, *In De Interp.*, ed. secunda, Meiser, 234.

[59] Simplicius, *In Cat.*, ed. Kalbfleisch, 195–196.

[60] Alexander, *In An. Pr.*, ed. Wallies, 184.

[61] Alexander inserts it to differentiate Philo's view from that of Aristotle, which was, according to Alexander, intermediate between the views of Diodorus and Philo: "The possible is that which is capable of coming into being and is not prevented, even if it does not come into being."

[62] Philoponus, *In An. Pr.*, ed. Wallies, p. 169, lines 19 ff.

[63] Cicero, *De Fato*, 12. See Zeller, *op. cit.*, vol. 3, part 1, p. 110, note 2.

that Cypselus rule at Corinth, even though the oracle had asserted this a thousand years before. For something to be possible it was only required that it be "capable of being." This seems to be essentially the same as Philo's theory.

Perhaps the account given at Diogenes Laertius, *Vitae* VII, 75, represents the view of Chrysippus.[64] According to this, some propositions are possible, some impossible, some necessary, some nonnecessary. A possible proposition is that which "*admits* of being true, when external events do not prevent its being true"; for example, "Diocles is living." An impossible proposition is one that does not admit of being true; for example, "The earth is flying." A necessary proposition is one which, being true, does not admit of being false, or admits of being false but is prevented by external circumstances; for example, "Virtue is beneficial." A nonnecessary proposition is one which is true and is capable of being false, the external circumstances not preventing it, such as "Dion is walking." This strongly resembles Philo's view, but is expressly distinguished from it and is characterized as the Stoic theory.[65]

As we shall now see, the different ways of interpreting conditional propositions were closely connected with the various views about necessity and possibility.

[64] Plutarch, *De Stoic. Repugn.*, chap. 46, p. 1055d, may be interpreted as indicating that Chrysippus held this view. Note the similarity of the example to Chrysippus' example in Cicero, *De Fato*, 12.

[65] Boethius, *In De Interp.*, ed. secunda, Meiser, 234–235.

CHAPTER IV

PROPOSITIONAL CONNECTIVES

SUMMARY

THE STOICS gave truth-functional definitions of all the more important propositional connectives, and defined also some non-truth-functional connectives. These definitions, and the various controversies over them, form the subject matter of the present chapter. The first section, on implication, contains an account of the four-sided argument over the truth-conditions for hypothetical propositions. It is shown that Philo's type of implication was exactly the same as the modern "material implication." Diodorean implication is defined and distinguished from Chrysippean implication, which is the ancient equivalent of what is now called "strict implication." The connection between Diodorus' views on implication and on necessity is shown. In the second section we are concerned with disjunction. The Stoics distinguished between inclusive and exclusive disjunction, gave truth-functional definitions of both types and also a non-truth-functional definition of the latter type. The third section considers conjunction, along with several other connectives. In the fourth section, we see how implication was defined in terms of conjunction and negation; also, how exclusive disjunction was defined in terms of negation and equivalence. Certain difficulties in the evidence for these definitions are pointed out.

§ 1: IMPLICATION

It seems that questions of logic were taken very seriously in ancient times. When Diodorus Cronus was unable immediately to solve a logical puzzle proposed to him at a royal banquet in Alexandria, he died in despair.[1] Philetas of Cos, another logician, was a victim of the famous antinomy of The Liar, as we know from his epitaph:

> Philetas of Cos am I
> 'Twas The Liar who made me die,
> And the bad nights caused thereby.[2]

Likewise the problem of the truth-conditions of conditional propositions, though it apparently caused no fatalities, inspired so much discussion in Alexandria that Callimachus reports, "Even the crows on the roof tops

---

[1] Diog. L., *Vitae* II, 111.
[2] *Athen.* IX, 401C (trans. Stock, *Stoicism*, p. 36).

are cawing about the question which conditionals are true."[3] It is indeed
a pity that so few results of all this discussion have been preserved.

In this section we shall investigate what remains of the ancient treatment of the problem just mentioned. We know that the controversy was
begun by Diodorus and Philo in the Megarian school and was taken up
and enlarged by the Stoics. Most of the latter seem to have adopted the
position of Philo,[4] although at least three other views were represented.
In modern times, C. S. Peirce was the first competent logician to comment on the ancient dispute.[5] He was struck by the fact that Philo's
notion of implication was exactly the same as the modern so-called "material implication," which also has provoked much debate. Other authors
have mentioned this same point of similarity,[6] and today it is probably
the best-known fact about Stoic logic.

We begin by repeating the definition of a conditional (συνημμένον): it
is a molecular proposition compounded by means of the connective "if."
For example, "If it is day, it is day"; or, "If it is day, it is light."[7] This
connective asserts that the second logically follows from (ἀκολουθεῖν) the
first;[8] but it is precisely the question of finding a correct criterion for this
"following" that raised so much controversy in the Stoic school.[9] Paren-
thetically it may be said that there is no doubt that the term "conditional" (συνημμένον), which was apparently first used in this technical
sense by Chrysippus,[10] retained its technical sense throughout the history
of Stoic logic. *Nowhere* in the Stoic fragments is the term applied to an
argument or an inference-schema; *all* examples given by ancient authors
to illustrate the meaning of συνημμένον are conditional propositions. *All*
the definitions of the term—and there are many of them—agree that a
conditional is a proposition, not an argument.[11]

Philo's position in the ancient argument was that a conditional is true
when and only when it does not have a true antecedent and a false con-

---

[3] Sextus, *Adv. Math.* I, 309–310. Callimachus was one of the most celebrated
Alexandrine grammarians and poets. He was chief librarian of the great library from
260 B.C. to 240 B.C. Eratosthenes and Apollonius of Rhodes were among his pupils.
References to the debate appear at Cicero, *Acad. II*, 143; Sextus, *Adv. Math.* VIII,
113 ff.; *Hyp. Pyrrh.* II, 110.
[4] *Hyp. Pyrrh.* II, 104; *Adv. Math.* VIII, 245.
[5] *Collected Papers*, vol. 2, p. 199; vol. 3, pp. 279–280.
[6] See, for example, the articles by Hurst, Chisholm, Łukasiewicz ("Zur Geschichte
der Aussagenlogik"), Bocheński (*De Consequentiis*, p. 3), and Reymond. See also De
Lacy, *Philodemus: On Methods of Inference*, p. 159, note 8; Stock, *op. cit.*, pp. 22–23;
A. Tarski, *Introduction to Logic* (New York, Oxford, 1941), p. 27, note 3; W. V.
Quine, *Mathematical Logic* (New York, Norton, 1940), p. 18.
[7] Sextus, *Adv. Math.* VIII, 109.
[8] Diog. L., *Vitae* VII, 71.
[9] *Adv. Math.* VIII, 112.
[10] Galen, *Opera*, ed. Kuhn, XI, 499 (*SVF* II, 212).
[11] See chap. vi, § 2.

sequent;[12] that is, a conditional holds unless its antecedent is true and its consequent is false.[13] This definition, which is perfectly familiar to logicians, apparently sounded paradoxical to some people in those days, as indeed it does to some now. It is accordingly repeated in full at many places in the fragments, and there are many examples.[14] Sextus offers for the combination (TT), "If there are gods, then the universe is conducted according to divine foresight"; for (FF), "If the earth is flying, then the earth has wings"; for (FT), "If the earth is flying, then the earth exists"; and for (TF), "If he is moving, then he is walking"—provided, says Sextus, he is moving but not walking.[15] Diogenes, who also was presumably following a Stoic handbook, gives a similar group of examples: for (TT), "If it is day, it is light"; and for (FF), "If it is night, it is dark" —both supposing that it is day. For (FT) he gives, "If the earth flies, then the earth exists"; and for (TF), "If the earth exists, the earth flies."[16]

These definitions and examples show clearly that Philonian implication is the same as what is now called "material implication." The truth-table itself was anticipated, as may be seen from the following passage:

Since, then, there are four possible combinations of the parts of a conditional—true antecedent and true consequent, false antecedent and false consequent, false and true, or conversely true and false—they say that in the first three cases the conditional is true (i.e., if the antecedent is true and the consequent is true, it is true; if false and false, it again is true; likewise, for false and true); but in one case only is it false, namely, whenever the antecedent is true and the consequent is false.[17]

Even the order of listing the cases seems to have been conventional, for we always find (TT), (FF), (FT), (TF).

Diodorus, however, declared that a conditional proposition is true "if it neither is nor ever was possible for the antecedent to be true and the consequent false."[18] To differentiate this view from that of Philo, Sextus gives a group of three critical examples:

(1)   If it is day, then I am conversing.
(2)   If it is night, then I am conversing.
(3)   If it is night, then it is day.

Now suppose that it is day and I am conversing. Then, according to Philo, (1) is a true conditional, since both its antecedent, "It is day" and

---

[12] *Adv. Math.* VIII, 112.

[13] *Ibid.*, 332.

[14] *Ibid.*, 113 ff., 245 ff., 333, 378, 449; *Hyp. Pyrrh.* II, 104 ff.; *Vitae* VII, 81.

[15] *Adv. Math.* VIII, 245; III, 16–17.

[16] *Vitae* VII, 81 ff.

[17] *Adv. Math.* VIII, 247.

[18] *Ibid.*, 115 ff. This passage and the passage in *Hyp. Pyrrh.* II, 110 ff., constitute our best comparisons of the views of Philo and Diodorus on implication.

its consequent "I am conversing" are true. But Diodorus would not agree that under the present supposition the conditional is true. For it *is* possible that the antecedent be true and the consequent be false. To prove this he refers to the time "when it is still day but I have ceased to converse." Also it *was* possible for the antecedent to be true and the consequent false; the relevant time is the time "before I began to converse."[19] Thus Diodorus would reject (1), since it does not hold for all times. Likewise with respect to (2), Philo would regard this conditional as true in case it is day and I am not conversing, for the antecedent would be false and the consequent false. But Diodorus would regard (2) as false, since it is possible that its antecedent be true and its consequent false; this will occur "when night has come on and I am not conversing." Again, Philo would regard (3) as true if it is day, for its antecedent "It is night" would in that case be false, while its consequent "It is day" would be true. But Diodorus would not accept (3) either, because it is possible (when night has come on) for the antecedent to be true while the consequent is false.

By reference to the foregoing, along with our previous consideration of Diodorus' concept of necessity, we are in a position to give a fairly exact characterization of Diodorean implication. (An explicit statement of the evidence will follow.) A conditional holds in the Diodorean sense if and only if it holds *at all times* in the Philonian sense.[20] This may be expressed succinctly by the following equivalence where → represents Diodorean implication):

$$(F \rightarrow G) \equiv (t) \, (F(t) \supset G\,(t))$$

To take a particular example, this would indicate that "If [Diodorean] it is day, then it is light" holds if and only if "If [Philonian] it is day at t, then it is light at t" holds for every value of t. Thus (1) above fails because there is a value of t such that "If it is day at t, then I am conversing at t" is not a true Philonian conditional for that value. Likewise (2) fails because there is a value of t such that "If it is night at t, then I am convers-

---

[19] It *is* possible, because it will happen in the future; it *was* possible, because it happened in the past. Cf. the account of Diodorean necessity in the previous chapter. For the "neither was nor is possible" idiom, cf. *Hyp. Pyrrh.* II, 230.

[20] It must always be remembered that the antecedent and consequent of a Diodorean conditional are propositional functions, i.e., they tacitly contain a free time-variable, whereas the constituents of a Philonian conditional are propositions. Thus, corresponding to each Diodorean conditional, we have an infinite number of Philonian conditionals—one for each moment of time. The Diodorean conditional is true if all these Philonian conditionals are true; but if there is a time t such that the corresponding Philonian conditional for that t is false, then the Diodorean conditional is false. Note that at Sextus, *Adv. Math.* VIII, 245, it is asserted that Philonian implication is basic to all the other kinds, i.e., is the weakest type.

ing at *t*" is not a true Philonian conditional. And in the same way, for
some (nighttime) value of *t*, "If it is night at *t*, then it is day at *t*" is false
in Philo's sense; and therefore "If it is night, then it is day" is false
according to Diodorus.

The evidence for this interpretation is as follows. Diodorus says that
a conditional holds if and only if two requirements are satisfied: (1) it *is*
not possible that the antecedent be true and the consequent be false,
and (2) it *was* not possible that the antecedent be true and the consequent
be false. Referring to the Diodorean definition of "is impossible" we find
that condition 1 informs us that the negation of the conditional does not
now hold in the Philonian sense, and will not so hold in the future. Condition 2 adds that the negation of the conditional did not so hold in the
past, either. Thus, if conditions 1 and 2 are satisfied—indeed, condition 2
is sufficient by itself, but would sound paradoxical—the negation of the
conditional did not, does not, and will not hold. So, in order that a conditional hold in the Diodorean sense, the same conditional with "at *t*"
added to each member must hold in the Philonian sense for all values of
t—past, present, and future.[21] Consequently, Diodorean implication may
be regarded as a special type of what Russell calls "formal implication."

We may verify this interpretation by considering again Diodorus'
reasons for not accepting "If it is day, then I am conversing" as a true
conditional. He gave two reasons, and clearly each was to be regarded as
sufficient. He first pointed out that at some time in the *future* the conditional would have a true antecedent and a false consequent (and thus
would be Philonian-false); he then added that at some time in the *past*
the conditional had a true antecedent and a false consequent. It was thus
made clear that if the conditional *ever*—past, present, or future—had a
true antecedent and a false consequent, Diodorus would not regard it as
true.

It is interesting to observe how Frege deals with the sort of conditionals
considered by Diodorus. Frege notices that a reference to time is tacitly
present in the clauses of these sentences and that they are not, properly
speaking, conditionals at all. To show this, Frege considers the example:
"If the sun is in the Tropic of Cancer, then we have (in the northern
hemisphere) the longest day." The sense of the antecedent here is not
a proposition, according to Frege, for if I say, "The sun is in the Tropic

---

[21] If the reader will consult *Adv. Math.* VIII, 415 ff., he will see that an example of
Diodorean implication is there under discussion. An attempt is made to show that
the conditional corresponding to the given argument is Diodorean-true. This is done
by showing that it never (μηδέποτε) has a true antecedent and a false consequent, for in
the day it has the combination (FF), and at night it has (TT). For "always" true,
the word ἀεί is used. For "sometimes," the word ποτέ is used.

of Cancer," the verb "is" refers to my present time, whereas in the conditional sentence the antecedent has no such reference. Similarly with the consequent. Thus the conditional in question does not properly express a molecular proposition. From this we may gather that Frege would not have considered his example to be true unless, for every *t*, If the sun is in the Tropic of Cancer at *t*, then we have at *t* the longest day, and so on.[22] This shows at least that there are certain common "if . . . then" sentences which received a Diodorean analysis at the hands of a very eminent mathematician and logician. Schröder also was puzzled by the apparent essential involvement of the notion of time in hypothetical propositions.[23] But a thoroughgoing Diodorean approach to propositional logic has not yet been carried out and possibly never will be.

Is Diodorean implication the so-called "strict implication" of C. I. Lewis? It is doubtful that any modern logician would recognize it as such; but one would probably get a different opinion from Diodorus, could *he* be consulted. For, according to Diodorus, whatever is true for all time is necessarily true; thus, any conditional which would satisfy his requirements for truth would also satisfy his requirements for necessary truth.[24]

The Stoic controversy over implication was by no means restricted to the Philonian and Diodorean views. In a very interesting and important passage Sextus states and illustrates four distinct definitions which were discussed by the Stoics. He arranges these from the weakest (material implication) to the strongest, and at each step cleverly finds an example which is true in all preceding senses but which is false in the sense at hand. The passage deserves quotation (numbers have been inserted to demarcate the different views more clearly):

[1] For Philo says that a true conditional is one which does not have a true antecedent and a false consequent; e.g., when it is day and I am conversing, "If it is day, then I am conversing"; [2] but Diodorus defines it as one which neither is nor ever was capable of having a true antecedent and a false consequent. According to him, the conditional just mentioned seems to be false, since when it is day and I have become silent, it will have a true antecedent and a false consequent; but the following conditional seems true: "If atomic elements of things do not exist, then atomic elements of things do exist," since it will always have the false antecedent, "Atomic elements of things do not exist," and the true consequent, "Atomic elements of things do exist." [3] And those who introduce "connection" or "coherence" say that a

---

[22] Frege, "Ueber Sinn und Bedeutung," pp. 43–44.

[23] E. Schröder, *Vorlesungen über die Algebra der Logik* (Leipzig, Teubner), vol. 2 (1891), sec. 28.

[24] Cf. C. I. Lewis and C. H. Langford, *Symbolic Logic* (New York, Appleton-Century, 1932), pp. 122, 124: " '*p* implies *q*' or '*p* strictly implies *q*' is to mean 'it is false that it is possible that *p* should be true and *q* false.' " See also C. I. Lewis, *Survey of Symbolic Logic* (Berkeley, University of California Press, 1918), p. 239.

conditional holds whenever the denial of its consequent is incompatible with its antecedent; so that, according to them, the above-mentioned conditionals do not hold, but the following is true: "If it is day, then it is day." [4] And those who judge by "suggestion" declare that a conditional is true if its consequent is in effect included in its antecedent. According to these, "If it is day, then it is day," and every repeated conditional will probably be false, for it is impossible for a thing itself to be included in itself.[25]

The example of Diodorean implication cited in this passage indicates that the ancients were aware that Diodorean as well as Philonian implication had its paradox, namely, that a proposition which is "always false" implies any proposition, even its own negation. The third type of implication, depending upon the incompatibility of the negation of the consequent with the antecedent, is thought to have represented the standpoint of Chrysippus.[26] A question may be raised in regard to the meaning of "incompatible." Judging from the position of this type in the list, which obviously was intended to proceed from weakest to strongest,[27] we are led to suppose that "incompatible" is used in its ordinary sense, according to which incompatible propositions *cannot* both be true, i.e., their conjunction is logically false. The example bears out this interpretation.

In Diogenes, also, there is a passage which may refer to the third type of implication.[28] He says, "Thus a true conditional is one in which the contradictory of the consequent is incompatible with the antecedent . . . a false conditional, on the other hand, is one in which the contradictory of the consequent is compatible with the antecedent." As an example of a true conditional he gives, "If it is day, it is light," and asserts that "It is not light" and "It is day" are incompatible. Now this conditional may have been regarded as analytic; if so, Diogenes' source refers to the third type of implication. The conditional may, however, have been considered as expressing a natural law; in this case Diogenes' source would perhaps have reference to Diodorean implication. An example of a false conditional is given also: "If it is day, Dion is walking." With regard to this, Diogenes says that "Dion is not walking" and "It is day" are perfectly compatible; again it seems clear that he means something else than that both are true, for he makes no provision to this effect. Probably he means that both propositions *might* be true, in some sense of "might." Finally, it should be noticed that the conditions given by Diogenes for

[25] Sextus, *Hyp. Pyrrh.* II, 110.

[26] Hurst, "Implication in the Fourth Century B.C.," p. 491; Zeller, *Die Philosophie der Griechen*, vol. 3, part 1, p. 105, note 5. I myself cannot find much evidence one way or the other.

[27] The examples make it obvious.

[28] Diog. L., *Vitae* VII, 73.

the validity of an argument correspond closely with those which he gives for the truth of the conditional.[29] This is further evidence for the view that the third type of implication is the ancient version of strict implication.

Concerning the fourth type, there is little to say beyond what appears in the passage quoted. As far as is known to the present writer, no further mention of this type is to be found in ancient literature. From Sextus' statement that the fourth criterion probably cuts out the duplicated propositions, which are ascribed to the Stoics by all our sources (including the Aristotelian commentators), and of which the Stoics seem to have been quite fond, we may conjecture that the fourth criterion was not adopted by any large group in the Stoic school.

The following is offered as a summary and interpretation of the four types of implication. Suppose that the Leibnizian distinction between the actual world and the possible worlds can be maintained. Then a Philonian conditional is true if either the consequent or the negation of the antecedent holds in the actual world. Diodorean implication holds between the members of a conditional which is always true of the actual world: "If it is day, then the sun is over the earth," to use a Stoic example. But this might not be true of all possible worlds. Chrysippean implication is that which holds between the members of a conditional which is logically true, that is, true of all possible worlds. The fourth type of implication seems to be a restricted type of Chrysippean implication and will have no special explanation by reference to the Leibnizian metaphysics.

There have been various other interpretations of Diodorean implication, and we should at least consider these briefly. Among the several authors who assert or suggest that Diodorean implication was the ancient counterpart of strict implication, only Martha Hurst[30] and Roderick Chisholm[31] present any evidence. Miss Hurst considers the hypothesis that Diodorus defined a true conditional as that which did not admit and does not admit of falsehood; according to her, this would simply be "that which, as a matter of fact, is always true." This hypothesis, which seems to correspond to that of the present writer, is rejected by Miss Hurst on the following grounds:

The objection to this interpretation of Diodorus is that it does not make his position in essentials at all different from Philo's. His criterion of "following" would have, in comparison with Philo's, the advantage of not being variable in application in the

[29] *Ibid.*, 77.
[30] Hurst, *op. cit.*
[31] Chisholm, "Sextus Empiricus and Modern Empiricism."

sense of covering and not covering the same example at different times, but it would have the disadvantage of never being applicable with certainty. This, for instance, would be a true case of "following," as far as we know: "If the sun sets in the west, the swallows fly south in Autumn." We have no certainty, however, that this is really a true case of following, for the consequent may be falsified next Autumn. Necessity and impossibility would have no meaning different from the meaning of truth and falsehood, and the views of Diodorus and Philo would coincide to the extent that both present a logic of two truth-values.[32]

These considerations, although interesting, are indecisive in regard to what Diodorus meant. It is perhaps true that according to this hypothesis no conditional could certainly be known to hold. But does this per se rule out the hypothesis? Miss Hurst thinks that it does, since Diodorus mentions a conditional which was true in his sense. But this probably shows only that Diodorus did not believe that propositions of fact cannot be known with certainty. And with reference to the conditional in question, Diodorus says that it is true because the antecedent is *always* (ἀεί) false.[33]

Miss Hurst is troubled by the temporal references in Diodorus' definition and in all the examples: "It may seem that in stressing the temporal aspect Diodorus has missed the main point, and that he attached too much importance to this is shown by the use of the two tenses in his own definition."[34] But she decides that these references are both "unfortunate and unnecessary."[35] However, her argument leading to these conclusions seems to me to contain a crucial mistake. She translates Diodorus' example of a true conditional in such a way as to make its antecedent the negation of an analytic sentence: "The elements of the existent are not without parts," whereas it should be, "There do not exist atomic elements of things."[36] Further, one must not overlook the Diodorean notions of necessity and possibility, in which the reference to time is clear indeed. Diodorus' definitions of these notions make it probable that the temporal references in the present example are not accidental.

[32] Hurst, *op. cit.*, p. 488.

[33] The conditional was, "If atomic elements of things do not exist, then atomic elements of things do exist." Even today, authors of texts on logic do not hesitate to offer examples of true sentences and of false sentences, even though philosophers have argued that no sentence can certainly be *known* to be true.

[34] Hurst, *op. cit.*, p. 486.

[35] *Ibid.*, p. 487.

[36] Neither Fabricius, Bekker, Mutschmann, nor Bury reads the text as Miss Hurst would have it (*ibid.*, p. 469). Further, the antecedent cannot be the negation of an analytic statement. For we are explicitly told that the denial of the consequent is not incompatible with the antecedent. Since the denial of the consequent *is* the antecedent, this implies that the antecedent is not incompatible with itself. But if the antecedent were the negation of an analytic statement, it would be incompatible with itself.

Professor Chisholm, in an otherwise excellent article, joins Miss Hurst in supposing that Diodorus was the ancient representative of C. I. Lewis. He quotes the following passage (Loeb translation): "And those who introduce 'connexion,' or 'coherence,' assert that it is a valid hypothetical syllogism whenever the opposite of its consequent contradicts its antecedent clause,"[37] and says of it, "This is what implication must be according to the Diodorans." But the reader will recognize this passage as the third part (and not the second) of the passage quoted on pages 47–48 above. Thus Sextus, who is our major source of information about the entire matter, sharply distinguishes this type of implication from that advocated by Diodorus. Further, in another part of his explanation of Diodorus' view, Chisholm says that Diodorus argued as follows:

But in addition to this, if we are to avoid the paradox of a false proposition implying any proposition, whether true or false, we must add that *a true implication* "will not reside either in that which begins with falsehood and ends in falsehood or in that which (passes) from falsehood to truth. Thus it only remains for it to exist in that which both begins with truth and ends in truth."[38]

But if the reader will consult the context from which the quoted passage is taken, he will see that Diodorean implication is not under discussion. The subject of the verb "will not reside" is "a signal"; and the topic of discussion at the place cited is the Stoic definition of "indicative signal."[39] Thus the passage does not throw any light on the nature of Diodorean implication.

§ 2: Disjunction

There seems to have been a corresponding controversy over disjunction, but unfortunately we do not know the details of this argument.[40] Matters stood somewhat as follows. Two basic types of disjunction were recognized by the Stoics: exclusive and inclusive. Exclusive disjunction (διεζευγμένον) was most used, and is the only type of disjunction which occurs in the five fundamental inference-schemas of Stoic propositional logic. It is clearly distinguished from inclusive disjunction (παραδιεζευγμένον), which, as its Greek name suggests, was regarded as somehow deficient in the qualities a disjunction ought to have.

Concerning the correct definition of exclusive disjunction, apparently there were at least two opinions. According to one,[41] an exclusive dis-

---

[37] Chisholm, *op. cit.*, p. 383; Sextus, *Hyp. Pyrrh.* II, 111. The passage cited contains a Bury mistranslation of συνημμένον.

[38] Chisholm, *op. cit.*, p. 382. The passage quoted by Chisholm is the Loeb translation of Sextus, *Adv. Math.* VIII, 249.

[39] See the Glossary, s.v. καθηγούμενον.

[40] Prantl, *Geschichte der Logik im Abendlande*, p. 460.

[41] Sextus, *Adv. Math.* VIII, 282.

junction is true when and only when just one member is true; or, as Diogenes puts it, an exclusive disjunction asserts that just one (τὸ ἕτερον) of its (two) component propositions is false.[42] This is the regular truth-functional definition, and it fits the fourth and fifth basic arguments.[43] According to these, if one supposes that a disjunction is given as true, one can argue from the truth of the first member to the falsity of the second, or from the falsity of the first to the truth of the second.[44] There were some among the Stoics who did not regard a disjunction as true unless the components were incompatible, i.e., unless the components could not both be true. For this we have the testimony of Gellius and Galen, and hints in certain remarks of Sextus. After giving the famous argument of Bias on marriage,

> Either you will marry a beautiful woman or you will marry an ugly one.
> If she is beautiful, you will share her with others.
> If ugly, she will be a punishment.
> But neither of these things is desirable.
> Therefore, do not marry.[45]

Gellius criticizes it on the grounds that the disjunction is not fair (*iustum*), since it is not necessary that one of the two disjuncts be true, "which is necessary in a disjunctive proposition."[46] In another place he argues similarly that the assertion of those who say "The commands of a father are either honorable or base" is not a true and regular disjunction (ὑγιὲς et νόμιμον διεζευγμένον) and lacks the third member, "or are neither honorable nor base."[47] In still another passage Gellius makes it even more clear that the Stoic logic with which he had come in contact must have propounded a non-truth-functional type of disjunction:

> There is also another, which the Greeks call διεζευγμένον ἀξίωμα [disjunctive proposition] and we call *disiunctum*. This is of such a sort as "Pleasure is either good or bad or neither good nor bad." All the disjuncts ought to be incompatible with one another, and their contradictories (which the Greeks call ἀντικείμενα) ought also to be incapable of being simultaneously true. Of all the disjuncts, one ought to be true, and the others false. But if none of them is true, or all, or more than one; or if the disjuncts are not incompatible, or if their contradictories are not contrary, then that disjunction is false.[48]

Galen reports that what the ancients called "discontinuous hypo-

---

[42] Diog. L., *Vitae* VII, 72.

[43] See chap. v.

[44] In this connection the following has some interest: "Exclusive disjunction announces that if this, not that, and if that, not this" (*sic*). Apollonius of Alexandria, Περὶ Συνδέσμων, ed. Schneider, 222.

[45] Gellius, *Noctes Atticae* V, xi, 1–2.

[46] *Ibid.*, V, xi, 9.

[47] *Ibid.*, II, vii, 21.

[48] *Ibid.*, XVI, viii, 12–14.

thetical protases" are called "disjunctions" by the newer philosophers (i.e., the Stoics),[49] and are called "quasi-disjunctions" by Galen himself.[50] He also tells us that the parts of a discontinuous hypothetical protasis exhibit partial incompatibility.[51] This means that it is not possible for both parts to be true, though it is possible for both to be false. Galen contrasts this rather strange view with his own,[52] according to which the term "disjunction" is reserved for compound propositions having parts that are "completely incompatible," and cannot either both be true or both be false.[53] Since there is a serious confusion here between a disjunction and a true disjunction, probably nothing of great interest can be inferred from Galen's report.

We have also a passage in Sextus which may hint at a strong interpretation of disjunction: "The true disjunction announces that one of its terms is true and that the other is false or others are false with [μετά] incompatibility."[54] Unfortunately, the import of this remark is not clear, and there is nothing in the context to help our understanding of it, nor do we find any parallel passages in Sextus.

The Stoics undoubtedly knew of inclusive disjunction, although we possess no clear truth-functional definition of this connective. Galen says: "Also in some propositions it is possible not only for one part to hold, but several, or even all; but it is necessary for one to hold. Some call such propositions 'almost disjunctions,' since disjunctions, whether composed of two atomic propositions or of more, have just one true member."[55] In a Scholium to Ammonius we learn that a παραδιεζευγμένον is composed of parts that are not contradictory of one another: "Socrates walks or Socrates converses."[56] From Apollonius of Alexandria we hear that the παραδιεζευγμένον announces that one term, or also another term, or even all the other terms hold. It differs from exclusive disjunction, he says, in that the latter announces that only one term holds.[57] He also mentions that disjunction is commutative. For example, " 'Either it is day or it is night' does not differ from 'Either it is night or it is day.' "[58]

[49] Galen, *Inst. Log.*, 9.

[50] *Ibid.*, 12.

[51] *Ibid.* With this cp. Apollonius of Alexandria, *op. cit.*, 218 (*SVF* II, 176), where the parts of "It is day or it is night" are given as Stoic examples of propositions that are incompatible (μαχόμενοι).

[52] *Inst. Log.*, 8, 10, 32.

[53] *Ibid.*, 8.

[54] *Hyp. Pyrrh.* II, 191.

[55] *Inst. Log.*, 12.

[56] Printed in the Preface to Ammonius, *In An. Pr.*, ed. Wallies, xi–xii.

[57] Apollonius of Alexandria, *op. cit.*, 219, 222.

[58] *Ibid.*, 484, 493. The language "does not differ from" is not what we would like to think the Stoics would have used.

Gellius, too, mentions the παραδιεϛευγμένον, but what he says about it is so confusing that it casts doubt on his account and also on our under-standing of the term.[59] The term does not even occur in Sextus,[60] nor is it to be found in Diogenes' rather extensive discussion of connectives.

§ 3: CONJUNCTION AND THE OTHER LOGICAL CONNECTIVES

According to the Stoics, a conjunction (συμπεπλεγμένον) is a proposition compounded by means of the connective "and."[61] Galen complains that "the followers of Chrysippus, fixing their attention more on the manner of speech than on the things spoken about, use the term 'conjunction' for all propositions compounded by means of the conjunctive connectives, whether they are consequents of one another, or incompatibles."[62]

A conjunction is true if both parts of it are true.[63] If one or more parts are false, the whole conjunction is false. Gellius gives, as an example of a true conjunction, "Scipio was the son of Paulus and was twice consul and triumphed and was censor and was colleague in the censorship of L. Mummius." He points out, "If to all those true statements which I have made about Scipio I add 'and he overcame Hannibal in Africa,' which is false, the totality of the statements made conjunctively will not be true, because of this one false statement which is made with them."[64]

Thus conjunction is defined in the usual way as a truth-functional con-nective. Apparently there were in ancient times, as now, persons who thought that a conjunction with only one false member should not be considered wholly false.[65] Sextus records the Stoic answer:

. . . just as in daily life we do not say that a cloak is sound [holds] just because most of it is sound and only a small part is torn, but on the contrary we say that it is torn because of the small part that is torn—so also in the case of a conjunction that has one false conjunct and several true ones, the whole will be said to be false because of the one false part.[66]

An inferential proposition (παρασυνημμένον), according to Crinis in his *Ars Dialectica* (*apud* Diogenes), is a molecular proposition compounded by means of the connective "since" (ἐπεί) and consisting of an antecedent and a consequent.[67] For example, consider "Since it is day, it is light." This connective asserts that the second follows from the first and that the first is true.[68] But we do not know exactly what to make of this, since

[59] *Noctes Atticae* XVI, viii, 14.
[60] I have trusted the indices of Bekker and Fabricius.
[61] Diog. L., *Vitae* VII, 72.
[62] Galen, *Inst. Log.*, 11.
[63] Sextus, *Adv. Math.* VIII, 125; Epictetus, *Diss.* II, ix, 8.
[64] *Noctes Atticae* XVI, viii, 11.
[65] Sextus himself was one of these.
[66] *Adv. Math.* VIII, 128.
[67] *Vitae* VII, 71. Cf. Scholium to Ammonius, cited above, in note 56.
[68] *Vitae* VII, 71, 74.

we do not know to which type of implication the word "follows" here
refers. If it refers to Philonian implication, then "since" would represent
the same truth-function as "and." This may indicate that "follows"
does not refer to Philonian implication; unfortunately, we do not at
present have any further clues in regard to what it does mean.

A causal proposition is a molecular proposition compounded by means
of the connective "because." For example, "Because it is day, it is
light."[69] The first is *as it were* (οἱονεί) the cause of the second. Clearly,
this is not a truth-functional mode of composition.

Several other non-truth-functional connectives are mentioned by less
reliable sources. However, only negation, implication, disjunction, and
conjunction were used essentially in the well-established Stoic calculus
of propositions; the others are merely mentioned in lists.

§ 4: THE INTERDEFINABILITY OF THE CONNECTIVES

One of the most interesting properties of the logical connectives is their
definability in terms of one another. The discovery of this fact, sometimes
placed in the Middle Ages and sometimes even credited to Leibniz, must
be dated at least as early as 250 B.C.

Chrysippus, with reference to the (material) conditional, "If anyone
is born under the Dog Star, then he will not be drowned in the sea,"
recommends that it be expressed as a negated conjunction, "Not both:
someone is born under the Dog Star and he will be drowned in the sea."
He recommends this, incidentally, so that people will not be misled into
supposing that a true material conditional indicates a necessary connection in nature. Cicero, who tells the story, continues sarcastically:

... thus the physician will no longer propose what he is certain of in his art in this
fashion, "If *x*'s veins are thus agitated, then *x* has a fever," but rather, "Not both:
x's veins are thus agitated and *x* does not have fever"; likewise, the geometer will not
say, "Great circles on a sphere divide one another into halves," but rather, "Not both:
there are great circles on a sphere and these do not divide one another into halves."
What proposition is there which cannot in this way be changed from a conditional
[*conexe*] to a negated conjunction?[70]

From Galen we learn that the disjunction "Either it is day or it is
night" means the same as the conditional "If it is not day, then it is
night." The passage concerned, which is accepted by Łukasiewicz as
showing that the Stoics were aware of the definition $(p \lor q) \equiv (\sim p \supset q)$,
is as follows:

And such a proposition as "Either it is day or it is night" is called a "disjunctive
proposition" by the newer philosophers, but a "discontinuous hypothetical protasis"

[69] *Ibid.*, 72.
[70] Cicero, *De Fato*, 15, 16.

by the ancients. The discontinuous protasis seems to have the same meaning as such a statement as this: "If it is not day, then it is night," which, when it is said in a conditional form of speech, is called a "conditional" by those who pay attention only to the sounds, but a disjunction [διεζευγμένον] by those who pay attention to the nature of what is meant. Similarly, such a form of speech as "If it is not night, then it is day" is a disjunctive proposition by the nature of what is meant, but in speech it has the form of a conditional.[71]

But there is a serious difficulty here. The disjunction involved in this statement should be inclusive disjunction (παραδιεζευγμένον), but the word used by Galen is the Stoic term for exclusive disjunction (διεζευγμένον). The example, too, is a standard example of exclusive disjunction. Further, we may be sure that Galen is not referring to the Stoics in the phrase "those who pay attention to the nature of what is meant."[72]

The correct solution of this difficulty has been found by J. W. Stakelum, author of an excellent work on the logic of Galen.[73] He shows that it is the word "conditional" (συνημμένον) and not "disjunction" (διεζευγμένον) which is used in an unusual sense in this passage. For Galen says that there are three relations among states of affairs: (1) *incompatibility*, in those which never coexist; (2) *consequence* (ἀκολουθία), in those which always coexist; and (3) a relation to which he gives no special name and which holds for those which sometimes coexist and sometimes do not.[74] He says further that states of affairs are *completely incompatible* if it is impossible that they simultaneously coexist or fail to exist.[75] Also, Galen's examples show that he regards states of affairs as exhibiting *complete consequence* if one exists when and only when the other exists. From this we see that the conditions under which A and B are completely incompatible states of affairs are exactly the same as the conditions under which A and $\sim B$ are related by complete consequence. Evidently, therefore, the proposition being asserted is:

$$(p \underline{\vee} q) \equiv (\sim p \equiv q)$$

and "conditional" is being used for "biconditional." The example bears out this interpretation.[76] For "It is day" and "It is night" represent completely incompatible states of affairs. Therefore, "It is not night" and "It is day" represent states of affairs between which ἀκολουθία holds.

---

[71] *Inst. Log.*, 9. I have translated πρότασις by "protasis" instead of "proposition" in order to distinguish it from the Stoic term ἀξίωμα.

[72] *Ibid.*, 11. Galen expressly says that the followers of Chrysippus pay attention to the manner of speaking instead of to the things spoken about.

[73] *Galen and the Logic of Propositions*, pp. 48–53. See also pp. 73–74.

[74] *Inst. Log.*, p. 33, lines 19 ff.

[75] *Ibid.*, p. 9, lines 17 ff.

[76] *Ibid.*, p. 9, lines 5 ff.

Thus, the διεζευγμένον "Either it is day or it is night" is said to have the same meaning as the συνημμένον "If (and only if) it is not night, it is day."

It is doubtful whether these remarks by Galen indicate that the equivalence under discussion was known to the Stoics. He seems rather to be saying that what certain persons "who pay attention only to the sounds" call συνημμένον is called διεζευγμένον by certain other persons "who pay attention to the nature of what is meant." Now, who were these persons? Both terms, συνημμένον and διεζευγμένον, were technical Stoic terms, which might indicate that the two groups represented factions of the Stoics. Also, since Galen elsewhere says, "The followers of Chrysippus . . . fix their attention more on the manner of speech than on the things spoken about," there is some probability that the Chrysippean Stoics were one of the factions.

Chapter V

ARGUMENTS

Summary

This chapter consists of five sections. In the first, "argument" is defined as "a system of propositions composed of premises and a conclusion." A valid argument, according to the Stoics, is an argument such that the negation of its conclusion is incompatible with the conjunction of its premises. A true argument is a valid argument which has true premises, and a demonstration is a special kind of true argument. Another subclass of the valid arguments contains the so-called "undemonstrated" arguments; of these, five types were called "simple" and the innumerable others were called "nonsimple," or "derived." To achieve generality in their discussions of propositional logic the Stoics made use of inference-schemas containing the numerals "first," "second," and so on as propositional variables. The second section contains an exposition of the five basic undemonstrated argument-types, as they are described in some twelve sources. The third section discusses an important Stoic principle which is closely related to the so-called "deduction theorem." In the fourth section is an account of the Stoic method of deriving nonsimple undemonstrated arguments from simple ones; examples are considered in detail. Note is taken of the assertion of the Stoics that their propositional logic was complete. The fifth section describes the Stoic classification of invalid arguments and also considers briefly the famous paradox of The Liar, which was the subject of much Stoic writing. The classification is found to be poor, but the Stoic version of The Liar is stronger than the usual Epimenides paradox.

§ 1: Definition and Classification

An argument, according to the Stoics, is "a system composed of premises and a conclusion." This definition, like the definition of "proposition," must have been a matter of common knowledge, for a number of authors repeat it verbatim.[1] The general word for argument is λόγος, which unfortunately was also used for sentence.[2] The word λῆμμα (premise) is also

---

[1] Thus, at Sextus, *Hyp. Pyrrh.* II, 135: λόγος δέ ἐστι σύστημα ἐκ λημμάτων καὶ ἐπιφορᾶς; and at Diog. L., *Vitae* VII, 45: [The Stoics say] εἶναι δὲ τὸν λόγον αὐτὸν σύστημα ἐκ λημμάτων καὶ ἐπιφορᾶς; and at Sextus, *Adv. Math.* VIII, 301: λόγος δέ ἐστιν, ὡς ἁπλούστερον εἰπεῖν, τὸ συνεστηκὸς ἐκ λημμάτων καὶ ἐπιφορᾶς. Cf. *ibid.*, 386, 388. On ἐπιφορά as the technical Stoic term for conclusion, see the Glossary; the term συμπέρασμα, given by Philoponus as a Peripatetic term (see the Glossary), seems also to have been used in the Stoic handbooks.

[2] See chap. iii and also the Glossary, s.v. λόγος.

ambiguous in Stoic logic, sometimes referring to either premise of an argument, and sometimes being restricted to the major premise of a two-premised argument.[3] Whether these ambiguities were present in Chrysippus' time is difficult to determine. The premises (in the wide sense of the word) are those propositions which are agreed upon for the sake of establishing the conclusion, and the conclusion is the proposition which is established from the premises.[4] Thus, for example, in the following argument the last proposition is the conclusion and the others are premises:[5]

> If it is day, then it is light.
> It is day.
> Therefore, it is light.

There has been a tendency among certain expositors of Stoic logic to confuse arguments with conditional propositions. Nothing in the Stoic texts justifies this confusion. Of course there is a conditional proposition *corresponding* to every argument—the conditional having the conjunction of the premises as antecedent and the conclusion as consequent—but this conditional is by no means the same as the argument.[6] Arguments and molecular propositions are both compounded of propositions, but molecular propositions are put together by means of connectives, and arguments are not.

The Stoics classified arguments as valid or invalid. Valid arguments, in turn, they divided into true and false. Some true arguments were

---

[3] Diogenes tells us (*Vitae* VII, 76): "An argument, according to the followers of Crinis, is composed of a major premise [λῆμμα], a minor premise [πρόσληψις], and a conclusion [ἐπιφορά]." As an example he gives:

> If it is day, then it is light.
> It is day.
> Therefore, it is light.

He explains that the first proposition is the major premise, the second is the minor, and the last is the conclusion.

[4] Sextus, *Hyp. Pyrrh.* II, 136. Since not everything can be proved, some propositions must be assumed in any argument (*Adv. Math.* VIII, 367).

[5] Sextus, *Hyp. Pyrrh.* II, 136. (Cf. the example in note 3 above.) Similarly Galen (*Inst. Log.*, 3–4) defines premise and conclusion by reference to the following example:

> Theon is identical with Dion.
> Philo is identical with Dion.
> Things identical with the same thing are identical with each other.
> Therefore, Theon is identical with Philo.

He says that the last proposition is the conclusion (συμπέρασμα) and that the premises are those propositions from the assumption of which the conclusion is inferred. For another instance of this definition of "premise" see *Adv. Math.* VIII, 302.

[6] *Hyp. Pyrrh.* II, 113.

demonstrative and others were not. This classification will now be described in detail.

An argument is valid (*συνακτικός* or *περαντικός*) when the conditional proposition having the conjunction of the premises as antecedent and the conclusion as consequent is Diodorean-true.[7] Arguments not satisfying this requirement are invalid. This, however, need not be taken as the *definition* of validity but only as the statement of a property which belongs to all valid arguments. Sextus always describes it as the Stoic *criterion* for validity,[8] though of course he does not think that it is a very useful criterion. Diogenes defines a valid argument as an argument which is such that the negation of its conclusion is incompatible with the conjunction of its premises.[9] Since Diogenes says that a conditional is true if the negation of its consequent is incompatible with its antecedent,[10] one could infer the criterion of Sextus from Diogenes' remarks, if one overlooked the important distinction between Diodorean and Chrysippean implication.[11]

Valid arguments are further subdivided into those that are true and those that are false.[12] A true argument is an argument which is valid and which has true premises; a false argument is either invalid or has a false premise. Our sources express this in several different ways, but there is no real disagreement among them. Thus, Sextus says that an argument is true not only when there is a logically true conditional having the conjunction of the premises as antecedent and the conclusion as consequent, but also when the conjunction of the premises (which is the antecedent of the conditional) is true.[13] Diogenes says that an argument is true if it validly draws its conclusion from true premises, and that it is false if it is invalid or if at least one of its premises is false.[14] Sextus repeats Diogenes' statement almost word for word, and he adds the obser-

---

[7] *Ibid.*, 137; *Adv. Math.* VIII, 415.

[8] *Hyp. Pyrrh.* II, 145.

[9] *Vitae* VII, 77. Diogenes defines only the invalid argument explicitly; I have presumed that he would agree that a valid argument is one which is not invalid.

[10] *Ibid.*, 73.

[11] Of course, there is no reason to suppose that Diogenes made such an inference. Further, the distinction between Diodorean and Chrysippean implication is very real and creates a serious problem here. In any case, it is clear that no mere Philonian implication was meant, but that the antecedent and the consequent must necessarily be connected; the choice between Diodorean and Chrysippean implication then depends upon one's notion of necessity.

[12] *Hyp. Pyrrh.* II, 138. Note that this does not mean that all false arguments are valid.

[13] *Ibid.* Cf. *Adv. Math.* VIII, 421: "So the argument becomes true not when the conjunction only is true nor when the conditional only is true, but when both are true."

[14] *Vitae* VII, 79.

vation that consequently the conclusion of a true argument will be true.[15] Galen, in a discussion of sophisms, says, "That they are false is evident because their conclusions are not true . . . false arguments have either a false premise or a conclusion improperly drawn."[16] Sextus, too, occasionally decides that an argument is false on the grounds that its conclusion is false.[17]

Just as the true arguments form a subset of the valid arguments, so the demonstrative (ἀποδεικτικός) arguments are a subset of the true arguments. Some of the valid arguments, we are told, have conclusions that are pre-evident, and others have conclusions that are nonevident.[18] For example, these arguments have pre-evident conclusions:

> If it is day, it is light.
> It is day.
> Therefore, it is light.

> If Dion walks, Dion moves.
> Dion walks.
> Therefore, Dion moves.

"It is light" is just as apparent as "It is day," and "Dion moves" is just as apparent as "Dion walks." But the following argument has a non-evident conclusion:

> If sweat flows through the surface, the skin has intelligible pores.
> Sweat flows through the surface.
> Therefore, the skin has intelligible pores.

Further, of the valid arguments which have nonevident conclusions, some merely "proceed" to their conclusions (ἐφοδευτικῶς); others proceed "by way of discovery" (ἐφοδευτικῶς καὶ ἐκκαλυπτικῶς). This distinction, which

[15] The close similarity of the passages suggests a slight emendation which would help the sense of Sextus' text considerably. Diogenes, *loc. cit.*, says: ἀληθεῖς μὲν οὖν εἰσι λόγοι οἱ δι' ἀληθῶν συνάγοντες. The version of Sextus, *Hyp. Pyrrh.* II, 187, is: ἀληθεῖς δέ εἰσι λόγοι δι' ἀληθῶν ἀληθὲς συνάγοντες. οὐκοῦν ἀληθής ἐστιν αὐτῶν ἡ ἐπιφορά. Now it seems that the word ἀληθές might well be omitted from the Sextus version. For not only is it superfluous, since what follows validly from true premises must be true, but its presence at this point renders the next remark of Sextus redundant. However, the close similarity of the passages suggests that both Sextus and Diogenes were referring to closely similar Stoic handbooks, and it is possible that the redundant remark is due to Sextus, while the preceding definition was copied from the handbook. In any event, the logical content of the remark is not affected.

[16] Galen, *De Peccatorum Dignotione*, ed. De Boer, p. 50, lines 2 ff.

[17] *Adv. Math.* VIII, 415.

[18] For the whole discussion of demonstrative arguments, our sources, except as otherwise noted, are *Adv. Math.* VIII, 305–314; and *Hyp. Pyrrh.* II, 140–143.

is by no means clear, is supposed to be illustrated by the following example:

> If a god has told you that this man will be rich, he will be rich.
> This god [Zeus] has told you that this man will be rich.
> Therefore, this man will be rich.

In this argument, according to Sextus, we accept the conclusion not because of the force of the argument but because of our belief in the statement of the god. This, consequently, is an example of an argument that merely proceeds to its conclusion and does not "discover" it. But in the argument about the pores, the premises serve somehow to "discover" the conclusion to us. An argument of the latter kind is said to be demonstrative.

Thus a demonstrative argument is an argument that is true and serves to reveal a nonevident conclusion. Diogenes defines it more simply as "an argument which, by means of what is more clearly apprehended, concludes that which is less clearly apprehended."[19]

There are, therefore, three principal types of argument: the valid, the true, and the demonstrative. Of these, the demonstrative is always both valid and true; the true is always valid but not necessarily demonstrative; the valid is not necessarily true or demonstrative.[20] Sextus, as is his custom, offers critical examples to illustrate the three types and to distinguish them from one another. First, he says, suppose that it is day and consider the following argument:

> If it is night, it is dark.
> It is night.
> Therefore, it is dark.[21]

This argument is valid, according to him, for when the premises are granted, the conclusion follows. But it is not true, since it contains the false premise, "It is night" (or, as he says in another place,[22] since it leads to a false conclusion). Next, under the same supposition, consider the following argument:

> If it is day, it is light.
> It is day.
> Therefore, it is light.[23]

---

[19] *Vitae* VII, 45.
[20] *Adv. Math.* VIII, 412 ff., 424.
[21] *Ibid.*, 311.
[22] *Ibid.*, 415. Elsewhere (*Hyp. Pyrrh.* II, 139) Sextus considers the same example. He says that the argument is valid because the conditional proposition, "If (it is night and if it is night it is dark) then it is dark," is true, but that the argument is not true because the antecedent conjunction of the conditional is false, for it contains a false conjunct.

This argument is valid and is also true, but it is not demonstrative, since its conclusion is pre-evident. An example of an argument which besides being true is also demonstrative is the following:

> If she has milk in her breasts, she has conceived.
> She has milk in her breasts.
> Therefore, she has conceived.[24]

In this argument the conclusion is nonevident and is revealed by the premises.

There is another classification of valid arguments which seems more important than that just discussed. In this classification the term "demonstrative" (ἀποδεικτικός) has a far different meaning from that which it has in the contexts mentioned above. The term "undemonstrated" (ἀναπόδεικτος) has two senses, we are told, since it is used both of arguments that simply have not been demonstrated and also of arguments that do not need to be demonstrated "owing to its being immediately clear in their case that they are valid" (συνάγουσιν).[25] Arguments of the five fundamental types (and also, apparently, all arguments reducible to these types) were called "undemonstrated" in the latter sense of the term.

The undemonstrated arguments are further classified into those that are simple and those that are not simple. The simple arguments are such that their conclusions "follow immediately from their premises." Examples of these are arguments of the five basic types, which will be described in the next section. Undemonstrated arguments are called "nonsimple" if they are compounded of simple ones and must be analyzed into their components in order that their validity may become evident. Next, nonsimple undemonstrated arguments are divided into homogeneous and heterogeneous, depending on whether they are compounded from several instances of one type of simple argument or from instances of different types of simple argument.[26]

It is by no means clear what sense of "demonstrate" is involved in the Stoic term "undemonstrated" as applied to the basic arguments. But it is clear that it is not the same sense involved in the word "demonstrative." For an invalid argument would be nondemonstrative, but it would not be undemonstrated.[27] It also appears that the five basic argu-

---

[23] *Adv. Math.* VIII, 312; cf. 422.

[24] *Ibid.*, 423. Cf. *Hyp. Pyrrh.* II, 106; Aristotle, *An. Pr.*, 27; *Rhet. I*, 2, 18; Plato, *Menex.*, 237e.

[25] *Adv. Math.* VIII, 223. But at 228 this same characteristic is given as the differentiating characteristic of *simple* undemonstrated arguments. This is a great difficulty.

[26] *Ibid.*, 228–229. Examples of the various kinds of undemonstrated arguments are given in § 2.

[27] Conversely, the "milk" and "pores" arguments, which were examples of demonstrative arguments, are also examples of the type 1 undemonstrated argument.

ments are *not* called "undemonstrated" because they are axiomatic while
other arguments are proved with reference to them.[28] For the arguments
which are proved by reference to the five undemonstrated arguments
are also called "(nonsimple) undemonstrated" arguments.[29] Apparently
every argument reducible to the five basic arguments is an undemonstrated argument.[30]

Although it was asserted that the Stoic system was complete, it was
also asserted that not every valid argument is an undemonstrated argument. Diogenes calls an argument "syllogistic" if either it is one of the
five undemonstrated arguments or it is reducible, by means of one or
more meta-rules, to the undemonstrated arguments.[31] He then gives an
interesting example of an argument which is valid but which is not
syllogistic:

> "It is day and it is night" is false.
>
> It is day.
>
> Therefore, it is not night.

---

[28] This is in opposition to Łukasiewicz, "Zur Geschichte der Aussagenlogik," p. 117:
"Von den Schlussformeln werden die einen als 'unbeweisbar' betrachtet, also sozu-
sagen *axiomatisch* als richtig angenommen, die anderen werden auf die unbeweisbaren
zurückgeführt. Die unbeweisbaren Schlussformeln oder Syllogismen soll Chrysippos
aufgestellt haben. Es sind dies die folgenden fünf . . ." (he continues with a list of the
five undemonstrated argument-types). Cf. notes 30 and 31, and Zeller, *Die Philosophie
der Griechen*, vol. 3, part 1, p. 114, note 1.

[29] Sextus, *Adv. Math.* VIII, 228–229.

[30] I suppose that along with doubts that "undemonstrated" means what others
have supposed, I ought to offer an explanation of what it does mean. This I am unable
to do. However, I might conjecture the following. According to the Stoics, *apud* Sextus, an argument is valid if the corresponding conditional is Diodorean-true. Thus
there would be at least two classes of valid arguments: those whose corresponding
conditional is a tautology, and those whose corresponding conditional is Diodorean-
true but not tautologous. The first class of arguments would be the undemonstrated
arguments, including arguments of the five basic types and all arguments derivable
from these. The second class of arguments would consist of demonstrated arguments;
these would be valid, because their corresponding conditionals would be Diodorean-
true, but for some, at least, their validity would not be immediately evident, because
it would rest on an empirical proposition. Thus, supposing "If it is day, then the sun
is over the earth" is Diodorean-true though conceivably false, the following one-
premised argument would be an example of a demonstrated argument:

> It is day.
> Therefore, the sun is over the earth.

This of course is entirely conjecture. Diogenes, who does not give the Diodorean-
true requirement in connection with validity but whose remarks imply rather a
logically true requirement, seems not to apply the term "undemonstrated" to arguments which are derivable from the basic arguments. Assuming that both Sextus and
Diogenes were following Stoic handbooks, we find it quite likely that Sextus was
correct in saying that the differences of opinion about implication were generating
great confusion in Stoic doctrine.

[31] Diog. L., *Vitae* VII, 78–79. I conjecture that the θέματα referred to on page 78 are
such principles as the θεώρημα mentioned in Sextus, *Adv. Math.* VIII, 231, which is
clearly a kind of meta-rule. This will be discussed in § 4. But cf. Ammonius, *In An.
Pr.*, ed. Wallies, p. 68, line 14.

This passage also exhibits another difficulty about the word "undemonstrated."

There is no doubt that this is indicative of a Stoic distinction between the negation of a proposition and a statement that the proposition is false.[32]

Several of the fragments mention a dispute within the Stoic school over whether one-premised arguments (μονολήμματοι λόγοι) exist.[33] The view that there were no such arguments was maintained by Chrysippus and his followers. The latter tended to argue by appealing to the authority of their master, which provoked Sextus to remark, "One doesn't have to believe in the utterances of Chrysippus as though they were pronouncements of the Delphic oracle!"[34]

Antipater of Tarsus, who was head of the Stoic school *ca.* 150–130 B.C., led the group which stood for the existence of the single-premised arguments. Examples proposed were:

> It is day.
> Therefore, it is light.

If Diogenes shares Sextus' information that all arguments reducible to undemonstrated arguments are undemonstrated arguments, why does he make separate mention of "the undemonstrated arguments" and "those that are reducible to the undemonstrated arguments"? For "syllogistic," cf. Sextus, *Hyp. Pyrrh.* II, 149.

[32] Note that this argument is given by Diogenes as an argument which is neither undemonstrated nor reducible to an undemonstrated argument. It is therefore clear that Diogenes is not merely offering what he supposes to be an argument of the following form:

> Not both: Plato is dead and Plato is living.
> Plato is dead.
> Therefore, Plato is not living.

for he characterizes the latter argument as an *undemonstrated* argument (*Vitae* VII, 81). Thus it appears that the Stoics were able to distinguish between the negation of a proposition and the statement that the proposition is false.

Compare the argument mentioned by Alexander, *In An. Pr.*, ed. Wallies, p. 22, lines 17 ff.

> It is day.
> You say that it is day.
> Therefore, you tell the truth.

According to Alexander, this argument is valid but not syllogistic. Two further examples (*ibid.*, p. 345) are:

> Dion says that it is day.   Dion says that it is day.
> Dion tells the truth.   It is day.
> Therefore, it is day.   Therefore, Dion tells the truth.

Another interesting example of an argument that is valid but not syllogistic is:

> B follows from A.
> A.
> Therefore, B.

(Alexander, *In An. Pr.*, p. 373, lines 31–35.) See, further, Galen, *Inst. Log.*, p. 42, lines 18 ff.; and Sextus, *Hyp. Pyrrh.* II, 186.

[33] Sextus, *Adv. Math.* VIII, 443; *Hyp. Pyrrh.* II, 167; Apuleius, *In De Interp.*, ed. Oud., 272; Alexander, *In Top.*, ed. Wallies, 8. The lack of agreement is intepreted by Sextus as indicating that the Stoics did not know what they were talking about.

[34] *Adv. Math.* VIII, 443.

> You are breathing.
> Therefore, you are living.[35]

> You are seeing.
> Therefore, you are living.[36]

The opposition maintained that these should be filled out, and that the last example was an abbreviated form of the argument:

> If you are seeing, you are living.
> You are seeing.
> Therefore, you are living.[37]

Besides arguing among themselves about the nature of arguments, the Stoics argued about this with the other schools. They were taken to task by the Peripatetics for the so-called "duplicated arguments" and "tautologous inferences." Duplicated arguments (διφορούμενοι) were arguments with a duplicated conditional for a major premise:

> If it is day, then it is day.
> It is day.
> Therefore, it is day.

Tautologous inferences (ἀδιαφόρως περαίνοντες) were arguments such that the conclusion was the same as one of the premises. For example:

> Either it is day or it is light.
> It is day.
> Therefore, it is day.[38]

The Peripatetic objection to these was that nothing can be a syllogism which does not "preserve the use of a syllogism," which is "to make something clear which does not appear to be known, and to do this by means of what is known and clear."[39]

One last point, which ought to be mentioned before we turn to a consideration of the five simple types of undemonstrated argument, con-

---

[35] Alexander, *In Top.*, 8.
[36] Apuleius, *In De Interp.*, 272.
[37] *Ibid.* The general term for arguments which were valid but needed to be filled out was ἀμεθόδως περαίνοντες. Cf. Alexander, *In An. Pr.*, ed. Wallies, 21, 22, 68, 345. Cf. also p. 17, lines 11–12, where Alexander rejects one-premised arguments on the basis of the etymology of συλλογισμός.
[38] Alexander, *In Top.*, ed. Wallies, p. 10. Cf. Cicero, *Acad. II*, 96, for another example of a duplicated syllogism.
[39] Alexander, *In An. Pr.*, ed. Wallies, p. 9, lines 23–25; p. 10, lines 5 ff. Cf. also *ibid.*, p. 18, lines 14 ff.; Apuleius, *In De Interp.*, ed. Oud., 272.

cerns the definition of "mood." A mood (τρόπος) is a sort of outline (σχῆμα) of an argument. For instance, corresponding to the argument:

> If it is day, then it is light.
> It is day.
> Therefore, it is light.

we have the following mood:

> If the first, then the second.
> The first.
> Therefore, the second.[40]

Schemata were classed as valid (ὑγιές or συνακτικός) or invalid (μοχθηρός or φαῦλος) according as they correspond to arguments that are valid or not.[41] Sometimes argument-schemata—half argument and half schema— were used, in order to avoid lengthy and unnecessary repetitions:

> If Plato is alive, then Plato breathes.
> The first.
> Therefore, the second.[42]

It is to be observed that the ordinal numerals which occur in the schemata always take propositions, never classes, as values.

§ 2: The Five Basic Types of Undemonstrated Argument

According to the Stoics, there were five basic types of undemonstrated argument. These were called "undemonstrated" because they had no need of demonstration, "since their validity is immediately clear."[43] These were basic, it was maintained, because all other syllogistic arguments could be reduced to them, and because they were supposed to be assumed even in categorical syllogisms.[44] Cicero tells us that from these basic schemata the Stoics "generated innumerable inferences, which make up almost the whole of dialectic."[45] And Sextus says that if he can show that the five basic schemata are invalid, then the whole of

---

[40] Diog. L., *Vitae* VII, 76; Sextus, *Adv. Math.* VIII, 227, 216, 236–237; Galen, *Inst. Log.*, p. 15, lines 8–9.

[41] Sextus, *Hyp. Pyrrh.* II, 146, 147, 154; *Adv. Math.* VIII, 132, 413, 414, 429, 444.

[42] *Vitae* VII, 77. Cf. *Adv. Math.* VIII, 306:

> If sweat flows through the surface, the skin has intelligible pores.
> The first.
> Therefore, the second.

[43] *Adv. Math.* VIII, 223.

[44] *Vitae* VII, 79; *Hyp. Pyrrh.* II, 156–157.

[45] *Topica*, 57.

TABLE 2
Sources for the Stoic Undemonstrated Arguments

Arg. type	Sextus, A.M. VIII	Sextus, H.P. II	Diog. L., Vitae VII	Galen, Inst. Log.	Galen, Hist. Phil.	Cicero, Topica	Mart. Capella, Opera IV	Philoponus, In An. Pr.	Ammonian document	Miscellaneous
1	224. Desc.* Example† 227. Schema‡	157. Desc. Example	80. Desc. Schema	15. Desc. Schema	15. Desc. Example	54. Desc.	414. Desc. Example 420. Schema	244. Desc. Example	68. Desc. λογότροπος	Schol. to Ammonius, xi. Desc. and example
2	225. Desc. Example Schema	157. Desc. Example	80. Desc. Example (?)	15. Desc. Schema	15. Desc. Example	54. Desc.	415. Desc. Example 420. Schema	244. Desc. Example	68. Desc. Example	Galen, *Med. Graec. Opera* I 434 ff. Desc. and Example Alexander, *In Top.* 166. Desc. Boethius, *In De Interp.* 2d ed. 351. Schema Schol. to Ammonius, xi. Desc. and example
3	226. Desc. Example Schema	158. Desc. Example	80. Desc. Example	15. Desc. Schema 33. Desc. Example	15. Desc. Example	54. Desc.	416. Desc. Example 420. Schema	245. Desc. Example	68. Desc. Example	
4		158. Desc. Example	81. Desc. Example	15. Desc. Schema	15. Desc. Example	56. Schema	417. Desc. Example 420. Schema	245. Desc. Example	68. Desc. Example	Alexander, *In Top.* 175. Desc.
5		158. Desc. Example	81. Desc. Example	16. Desc. Schema	15. Desc. Example	56. Schema	418. Desc. Example 420. Schema	245. Desc. Example	68. Desc. Example	Alexander, *In Top.* 175. Desc.
Other						57. 6th mode schema 7th mode schema	6th mode 419. Desc. Example 420. Schema 7th mode 419. Desc. Example 420. Schema			

* The entry "Desc." refers to something like this: "A type I undemonstrated argument is an argument having a conditional and its antecedent as premises and the conditional's consequent as conclusion."

† The entry "Example" means that something like the following will be found at the place cited:

If it is day, then it is light.
It is day.
Therefore, it is light.

‡ The entry "Schema" means, for instance:

If the first, then the second.
The first.
Therefore, the second.

dialectic will have been overturned.[46] It thus appears that at least an important part of dialectic consisted of a kind of calculus, with the five basic argument-schemata taken as axiomatic and the other (nonsimple) undemonstrated argument-schemata proved on the basis of these five.

There is little doubt that the five basic types of undemonstrated argument were propounded by Chrysippus, who may or may not have originated them.[47] They played a very important role in ancient logic, being incorporated into the Peripatetic logic under the title "theory of the hypothetical syllogism." There was some controversy over the number of the basic arguments,[48] and two of our sources list more than five;[49] we are told that it was Chrysippus who insisted that there were only five.[50]

Our knowledge of the five basic arguments is more certain than that of any other feature of Stoic logic. Fortunately all five are listed in at least eight places (by seven, or possibly eight, authors); and, in addition, various subsets of the five are mentioned. The second undemonstrated argument is described in at least thirteen different passages (written by ten, or possibly eleven, different authors).[51] With one or two exceptions, the sources fully agree, and differ only in the completeness with which they discuss the various points. (See table 2.) Since, all things considered, the accounts of Sextus are the most detailed and clear, these will be followed in the exposition below.

A type 1 undemonstrated argument is that which, from a conditional and its antecedent, infers the consequent as a conclusion. "That is," says Sextus, "when an argument has two premises, of which one is a conditional and the other is the antecedent of the conditional, and also has as its conclusion the consequent of the same conditional, then such an argument is said to be a type 1 undemonstrated argument."[52] Sextus then offers and explains the following argument as an example:

If it is day, then it is light.	(the conditional)
It is day.	(its antecedent)
Therefore, it is light.	(its consequent)

[46] *Hyp. Pyrrh.* II, 156. How can Sextus be so foolish?

[47] They are ascribed to Chrysippus in many places: Sextus, *Adv. Math.* VIII, 223; Diog. L., *Vitae* VII, 79; Galen, *Inst. Log.*, 14, 33, 34. Prantl and Zeller suppose that the five argument-schemas were originally due to Theophrastus; as to this, Bocheński says: "Il fallait donc toute la précipitation et le manque de jugement de Prantl pour affirmer que notre logicien [Theophrastus] a inventé toute la liste des ἀναπόδεικτα et beaucoup d'autres thèses encore." *La Logique de Théophraste*, pp. 116–117. See chap. vii, note 5.

[48] *Vitae* VII, 79.

[49] Cicero, *Topica*, 57; Martianus Capella, *Opera*, IV, 414 ff.

[50] *Vitae* VII, 79. Cf. *Inst. Log.*, 32: "They [the Stoics] say that there is no sixth, seventh, eighth, ninth, nor any other [basic undemonstrated] syllogism."

[51] Depending on whether or not Galen is the same as Pseudo-Galen.

[52] *Adv. Math.* VIII, 224.

He adds that the schema is:

> If the first, then the second.
> The first.
> Therefore, the second.[53]

A type 2 undemonstrated argument is that which, from a conditional and the contradictory of its consequent, infers the contradictory of the antecedent as a conclusion. "That is, when an argument has two premises, of which the one is a conditional and the other is the contradictory of the consequent of the conditional, and also has as its conclusion the contradictory of the antecedent, then such an argument is a type 2 undemonstrated argument." Again an example is offered and explained in painstaking detail:

> If it is day, then it is light. (the conditional)
> It is not light.   (the contradictory of the consequent)
> Therefore, it is not day.   (the contradictory of the antecedent)

---

[53] Bury's translation of συνημμένον as "hypothetical major" is somewhat confusing, for there is nothing in the statement of Sextus to prevent the other premise from being a conditional, nor is there anything to prevent the premises from being interchanged. This applies also to Bury's translation of the remainder of both passages.

The examples offered by our various sources reveal that some of their authors were better logicians than others. Thus Sextus and Diogenes give examples which are perfectly to the point, but the commentators, who were trying hard to force the Stoic theory into an Aristotelian matrix, are not so clear. Philoponus offers:

> If what approaches is a man, it is an animal.
> But it is a man.
> Therefore, it is an animal.

The Ammonian scholiast gives:

> If man, then animal.
> But *A*.
> Therefore *B*.

These are very nearly versions of the syllogism in Barbara.

Hicks' translation of the schema for the type 1 undemonstrated argument shows that he, like the Aristotelian commentators, did not realize that the Stoics used ordinal numerals for propositions, not for classes:

> If the first, then the second.
> The first is.
> Therefore, the second is.

Cf. Prantl, *Geschichte der Logik im Abendlande*, vol. 1, p. 473, who commits the same error. This error, by the way, is not original with Prantl, as Łukasiewicz ("Zur Geschichte der Aussagenlogik," p. 113) seems to suppose, but goes back to an ancient confusion between "is" and "is true." Cf. Sextus, *Hyp. Pyrrh.* II, 148: . .,. ἐπαγγέλλεται τὸ συνημμένον ὄντος τοῦ ἐν αὐτῷ ἡγουμένου εἶναι καὶ τὸ λῆγον; *Adv. Math.* VIII, 111: ἐπαγγέλλεσθαι δὲ δοκεῖ τὸ τοιοῦτον ἀξίωμα ἀκολουθεῖν τῷ ἐν αὐτῷ πρώτῳˑτὸ ἐν αὐτῷ δεύτερον καὶ ὄντος τοῦ ἡγουμένου ἔσεσθαι τὸ λῆγον; Aristotle, *Meta.*, 1017a30 ff.

The schema is:

> If the first, then the second.
> Not the second.
> Therefore, not the first.[54]

A type 3 undemonstrated argument is an argument which, for its first premise, has the denial of a conjunction; for its second premise, one of the conjuncts; for its conclusion, the contradictory of the other conjunct. Thus, for example:

> Not both: it is day and it is night. (negated conjunction)
> It is day. (the first conjunct)
> Therefore, it is not night. (the contradictory of the other conjunct)

Its schema is:

> Not both the first and the second.
> The first.
> Therefore, not the second.[55]

---

[54] Something is the matter with the example given by Diogenes:

> If it is day, then it is light.
> It is night.
> Therefore, it is not day.

Probably the second premise, ἀλλὰ μὴν νύξ ἐστιν, should be οὐκ ἔστι δὲ φῶς or οὐχὶ δέ γε φῶς ἐστιν, as Sextus has. Cf. Diogenes' example for the type 5 undemonstrated argument. Galen's account (*Hist. Philos.*) was reconstructed by Diels (*Dox. Graeci*) on the analogy of Sextus, *Hyp. Pyrrh.* II, 157. Philoponus and the Ammonian document again give doubtful examples, and the scholiast to Ammonius goes entirely wrong with:

> If man, then animal.   If not animal, then not man.
> If not animal, then not man.   If man, then animal.

Showing the application of philosophy to medicine, there is the example by Galen (*Opera*, ed. Kuhn, I, 434–435):

> If man were one, then he would not have pains.
> He has pains.
> Therefore, he is not one.

The version of Martianus Capella contains a different arrangement of negatives:

> If not the first, then not the second.
> The second.
> Therefore, the first.

[55] Bury's translations of these passages are none too good, but Hicks' translation of the Diogenes passage contains a very serious error. The Greek is: τρίτος δέ ἐστιν ἀναπόδεικτος ὁ δι' ἀποφατικῆς συμπλοκῆς καὶ ἑνὸς τῶν ἐν τῇ συμπλοκῇ ἐπιφέρων τὸ ἀντικείμενον τοῦ λοιποῦ. Hicks translates thus: "The third kind of indemonstrable employs *a conjunction of negative propositions* for major premiss and one of the conjoined propositions for minor premiss, and concluding thence the contradictory of the remaining proposition" (italics mine). Cf. Galen, *Inst. Log.*, 10, where ἀποφατικὴ συμπλοκή is explicitly defined.

It would seem desirable that, besides avoiding gross errors like the one noted above, translators of the logical fragments should endeavor to remain very close to the text. Note, for instance, how superior a literal translation of the example at Diogenes, *Vitae* VII, 80, would be to the more colloquial translation given by Hicks.

A type 4 undemonstrated argument is that which, employing a disjunction (exclusive) as one premise and one of the disjuncts as the other, infers the contradictory of the remaining disjunct as its conclusion. The example given by Sextus is:

> Either it is day or it is night.
> It is day.
> Therefore, it is not night.

HICKS' TRANSLATION

> It is not the case that Plato is both dead and alive,
> But he is dead,
> Therefore, Plato is not alive.

LITERAL TRANSLATION

> Not both: Plato has died and Plato is living.
> Plato has died.
> Therefore, not: Plato is living.

The Greek version is an exact substitution-instance of the schema.

Cicero, in his account of the type 3 undemonstrated argument, seems to have been thinking of many-termed conjunctions, for he says, "When, on the other hand, you negate any set of conjuncts and assume one or more of these in order to negate what remains, the result is called 'the third mood of inference'." He later offers, as a sixth mood, the following:

> Not both this and that.
> This.
> Therefore, not that.

But all is not well with the text here, as is proved by the immediately following seventh mood:

> Not both this and that.
> Not this.
> Therefore, that.

which, of course, is absurd. Martianus Capella, who seems to have been following Cicero, gives the same sixth and seventh moods. He also gives an unusual version of the third mood:

> Not both the first and not the second.
> The first.
> Therefore, the second.

Philoponus and the Ammonian document give an example which is as inexact as Hicks' translation of Diogenes' example:

> That which approaches is not both a horse and a man.
> But it is a man.
> Therefore, it is not a horse.

Cf. also Galen, *Inst. Log.*, who gives the correct schema, but at the same time offers an inexact example:

> Dion is not both at Athens and at the Isthmus.
> He is at Athens.
> Therefore, he is not at the Isthmus.

The schema, which appears in the accounts of Diogenes, Galen, Cicero, and Martianus Capella, but not in that of Sextus, is:

> Either the first or the second.
> The first.
> Therefore, not the second.[56]

A type 5 undemonstrated argument is an argument which, having an exclusive disjunction and the contradictory of one of the disjuncts as premises, infers the other disjunct as its conclusion. For example:

> Either it is day or it is night.
> It is not night.
> Therefore, it is day.

The schema, to be found only in Galen (*Inst. Log.*), Cicero, and Martianus Capella, does not quite agree with the example, which occurs in Sextus, Galen (*Hist. Phil.*), and Diogenes:

> Either the first or the second.
> Not the first.
> Therefore, the second.

We possess a statement that the commutative law holds for disjunction, but whether this was taken as an assumption or was derived in the system we do not know.[57]

The most serious difficulty which arises in connection with the foregoing account is as follows. In all examples in which the word "contradictory" (ἀντικείμενον) appears we should expect to find "negation"

---

[56] The account given by Sextus at *Adv. Math.* VIII, 223 ff., which is by far the most careful and full account extant, considers only the first three undemonstrated arguments. It is clear that this is not merely a gap in the text. Probably Sextus was not interested in giving a full list at this point, since his purpose in mentioning the undemonstrated arguments was to show by analysis that a certain argument of Aenesidemus was syllogistic (223). Only the first three undemonstrated arguments were required for the analysis (229–238). In his other discussion of the undemonstrated arguments (*Hyp. Pyrrh.* II, 157 ff.), where his purpose is to show that the whole of dialectic rests on a poor foundation, Sextus lists all five of the basic arguments, though his discussions of them are briefer than those in *Adv. Math.*

[57] Apollonius of Alexandria, Περὶ Συνδέσμων, ed. Schneider, 218. Since there seems to be no ready way of deciding whether the example or the schema exemplifies the Stoic theory more correctly, or whether, due to some principle of commutativity, the problem does not even exist, I shall prefer the testimony of Diogenes and Sextus to that of Cicero (Galen lends support to both versions). On the whole, Cicero does not give as clear an account of any aspect of Stoic logic as does Sextus or Diogenes.

Further basic undemonstrated arguments were given by Cicero, as indicated in note 55 above. These cannot be regarded as creating a very serious problem, since (1) they do not make sense, (2) they are not mentioned by anyone else except Martianus Capella, who was probably copying from Cicero, and (3) we have express statements that the Stoics thought there were five and only five basic undemonstrated arguments. Cf. note 50.

(ἀποφατικόν)[58]—at least if the schemas are not to be considered erroneous. Thus, according to the description, the following would be a type 2 undemonstrated argument:

> If it is day, then it is not night.
> It is night.
> Therefore, it is not day.

But according to the schema, it would not.

Unfortunately, none of the examples given by our sources is decisive. The question at issue is essentially whether the Stoics assumed the principle of double negation. It can be said with fair certainty that the appearance of the word ἀντικείμενον is not accidental, for our sources agree on it.

§ 3: THE PRINCIPLE OF CONDITIONALIZATION

By a "principle of conditionalization" is here meant something like the following: If a conclusion β is validly derivable from the premises $a_1, a_2, \cdots, a_n$, then the conditional proposition $\ulcorner((a_1. a_2. \cdots. a_n) \supset \beta)\urcorner$ is logically true. In order that a principle of this sort have a precise meaning, it is necessary for the phrase "validly derivable" to have a precise meaning. Generally speaking, this phrase would be defined by reference to the inference-rules of the system of logic under consideration. Thus a principle of conditionalization can be considered a rule of inference, though an unusual one in that its statement will refer to the other rules and even to (prior applications of) itself.[59]

Now there are certain passages among the Stoic fragments which we may say are virtually statements of a principle of conditionalization, if we make the following important reservations: (1) the Stoics always state the principle as an equivalence instead of as a conditional; (2) the contexts in which the principle occurs are always contexts in which Sextus interprets the Stoics as trying to give a criterion for the validity of arguments; (3) "logically true" is replaced, usually, by "Diodorean-true"; and (4) there is no extant example of the Stoics' using the principle as a rule of inference. But these reservations should not cloud the interesting similarity between the Stoic principle and the modern rule.

---

[58] See the Glossary, s.v. ἀποφατικόν.

[59] Reference is made to Quine, *A Short Course in Logic*, chap. i; Gentzen, "Untersuchungen über das logische Schliessen," pp. 176–210, 405–431; and Jaskowski, "On the Rules of Suppositions in Formal Logic." Obviously this principle is closely related to the "deduction-theorem" of Tarski, except that no provisions about substitution need be made, since there is no rule of substitution. So also in Stoic logic, no substitutions can be made, for the Stoics did not regard expressions containing variables as sentences; i.e., no expression containing variables would ever appear in the statement of a Stoic argument.

The principle is described and referred to in many different places.[60] One of the best passages is Sextus, *Adv. Math.* VIII, 415 ff., a translation of which will be found in Appendix A. The reader will notice that, although there is no explicit reference to Diodorus, the treatment of the examples makes it probable that Diodorean implication is meant.[61] The first argument offered as an example is:

> If it is night, then it is dark.
> It is night.
> Therefore, it is dark.

The corresponding conditional is:

> If (it is night and if it is night, it is dark) then it is dark.

"But this conditional is true since it *never* has a true antecedent and a false consequent. For when it is day, the antecedent, namely, "It is night and if it is night, it is dark," is false, and its consequent, "it is dark," is false, and so the conditional is true. And at night it will have a true antecedent and a true consequent, and will therefore be true." In this quotation the word "never" seems clearly to refer to time, especially since the assertion is supported by showing that the conditional holds both when it is day and when it is night, that is, *always*. It is very doubtful that the Stoics regarded "Either it is night or it is day" as tautologous; compare the second premise of the paradox:

> If it is not night, then it is day.
> If nothing exists, then it is not night.
> Therefore, if nothing exists, then it is day.[62]

A few sections later, Sextus considers another example and again argues that the corresponding conditional never has a true antecedent and a false consequent, since this does not occur when it is day and does not occur when it is night.[63] He then gives an example of an invalid argument and proves it invalid by showing that the corresponding conditional will have a true antecedent and a false consequent when it is night. The argument is:

> If it is day, it is light.
> It is light.
> Therefore, it is day.

---

[60] Many scholars have not understood these passages because of their inability to follow the Stoic distinction between a valid argument and the corresponding true conditional.

[61] Heintz (*Studien* . . ., p. 196) is so certain of this that he even proposes to emend the text on the basis of it. See Appendix A, note 20.

[62] Alexander, *In An. Pr.*, ed. Wallies, p. 374, lines 25 ff.

[63] *Adv. Math.* VIII, 419.

The corresponding conditional, which is not Diodorean-true, is as follows:

> If (it is light and if it is day, it is light) then it is day.[64]

There are clear references to the same principle in *Adv. Math.*, and several other statements and references to it in *Hyp. Pyrrh.*[65] However, these statements are usually mistranslated, and few of the references would even be recognized by any reader not working with the original Greek. For instance, the reader of Bury's translation would find, ". . . the conclusive argument is non-apprehensible, for if it is judged by the coherence of the hypothetical premise, and the coherence in that premise is a matter of unsettled dispute . . .," which is certainly not a very clear reference to our principle, instead of ". . . the valid argument is non-apprehensible, for if it is judged by the logical truth of the conditional, and the logical truth of the conditional is a matter of unsettled dispute . . .,"[66] which is an unmistakable reference to the principle (as well as to the dispute over implication).

Since the conditionals corresponding to certain arguments, especially to those having a conditional as a premise, are rather unusual propositions and certainly not the sort of thing one would find very often in ordinary Greek,[67] one can readily understand how the text of Sextus has become corrupt in many of the places where these conditionals are mentioned. Fortunately, the task of reconstruction is relatively easy, since Sextus usually tells us that he is going to form a conditional proposition with such and such as antecedent and such and such as consequent; thus we are in effect given directions for reconstructing the mutilated passages. Besides, closely analogous passages have been corrupted in different ways; so we are left with different parts of the same barbarous conditional.[68]

The conditionalization principle is not to be found in Diogenes' account of Stoic logic. But Diogenes says that an argument is valid if and only if the negation of the conclusion is incompatible with the conjunction of the premises, and he also says that a conditional is true if and only if the negation of the consequent is incompatible with the antecedent.[69] Probably the Stoics agreed that an argument is valid if and only if the corresponding conditional is necessarily true, but they disagreed over the definition of "necessary." Some, following Diodorus, stated the principle

---

[64] *Ibid.*, 421–422; cf. Appendix A, note 17, for comment on text.
[65] Cf. the statements at *Hyp. Pyrrh.* II, 113, 137 (see Appendix A).
[66] *Ibid.*, 145 (Loeb trans., vol. 1, p. 245).
[67] E.g., "If [(if it is day then it is light) and (it is day)] then it is light" (*Hyp. Pyrrh.* II, 113).
[68] See my article, "Stoic Logic and the Text of Sextus Empiricus."

in such a way as to require that the conditional be always true; others, following the more usual notion of necessity, required that the conditional be necessarily true in their sense of "necessary." The criticism of Sextus (to the effect that the Stoic principle offered no practical criterion of validity because the Stoics had not agreed on the truth-conditions for conditionals) would still be germane.[70]

§ 4: THE ANALYSIS OF NONSIMPLE ARGUMENTS

By the "analysis" of an argument the Stoics meant the procedure of reducing the argument to a series of the basic undemonstrated arguments.[71] They had four general rules (θέματα) by which these analyses were to be carried out.[72] Unfortunately, our knowledge of these rules and of the exact manner in which they were applied is very deficient.

Apuleius[73] gives us an explicit statement of the first rule (τὸ πρῶτον θέμα). He says that the Stoics called it *prima constitutio* and *primum expositum* and that they put it as follows: "If from two propositions a third is deduced, then either of the two together with the denial of the conclusion yields the denial of the other."[74]

Thanks to Alexander and Simplicius[75] we also possess an explicit statement of the third rule (τὸ τρίτον θέμα): "If from two propositions a third is deduced and there are propositions from which one of the premises may be deduced, then the other premise together with these propositions will yield the conclusion."

In regard to the nature of the second and fourth rules, we are in the dark. However, Sextus mentions "a dialectical theorem [θεώρημα] that has been handed down for the analysis of syllogisms," which ran as follows: "If we have premises which yield a conclusion, then we have in effect also this conclusion among the premises, even if it is not explicitly stated."[76] There are strong reasons for regarding this θεώρημα as one of

---

[69] *Vitae* VII, 73, 76.
[70] *Hyp. Pyrrh.* II, 145; *Adv. Math.* VIII, 426–427.
[71] *Adv. Math.* VIII, 229, 230, 231, 235, 237, 240.
[72] For a list of the relevant fragments, see the Glossary, s.v. θέμα.
[73] *In De Interp.*, ed. Oud., 277–278.
[74] Note the similarity of this rule to the following inference-schema, which was proved by the Stoics:

> If the first and the second, then the third.
> Not the third.
> The first.
> Therefore, not the second.

[75] Alexander, *In An. Pr.*, ed. Wallies, p. 278, lines 6 ff.; Simplicius, *In De Caelo*, ed. Heiberg, p. 336, lines 33 ff. Cf. Alexander, *op. cit.*, p. 274, lines 19 ff.
[76] *Adv. Math.* VIII, 231.

the four θέματα; possibly it is merely another version of the third.[77] Sextus shows in some detail how this rule was used. Stated generally, the method was as follows. Suppose that a conclusion allegedly follows from certain premises and we wish to analyze the argument by means of our θεώρημα. We take the premises and deduce various conclusions from them by means of the five basic arguments; we then "add" these conclusions to the premises and repeat the procedure. Eventually, if the original argument was syllogistic, and if we are skilled enough, we shall deduce the conclusion. The number of unnecessary inferences made will depend upon the skill and practice of the person who makes the analysis.[78]

Sextus gives us two very clear examples of the analysis of an argument into its component basic arguments. These examples are closely parallel and should be read with reference to each other. The first argument to be analyzed is as follows:

  (1) If it is day, then if it is day it is light.
  (2) It is day.
       Therefore, it is light.

---

[77] These reasons are: (1) The general form and content of this θεώρημα is similar to that of the θέματα. (2) The θεώρημα is said to be a rule for the analysis of syllogisms, which is exactly the function ascribed to the θέματα. (3) The term θεώρημα is applied by Alexander to the Peripatetic version of the θέματα (though the θεώρημα we are considering is given by Sextus as a part of Stoic logic). (4) Even the phrase "*handed down*" for the analysis of syllogisms" is applied to both the θεώρημα and the θέματα.

We are told explicitly that the argument διὰ δύο τροπικῶν (whose schema we know) can be analyzed by means of the first and second θέματα. We are fairly certain that the rule given by Apuleius is the first θέμα. Thus, if the θεώρημα is the second θέμα, we ought to be able to analyze the argument διὰ δύο τροπικῶν by means of these two rules. This can be done as follows: by the first undemonstrated schema we have:

$$\frac{\begin{matrix}1 \supset \sim 2\\ 1\end{matrix}}{\sim 2}$$

Whence, by applying the first θέμα, we have:

$$\frac{\begin{matrix}1\\ 2\end{matrix}}{\sim (1 \supset \sim 2)}$$

Since this is syllogistic, the following is also syllogistic (in virtue of the θεώρημα):

$$\frac{\begin{matrix}1 \supset 2\\ 1\end{matrix}}{\sim (1 \supset \sim 2)}$$

From this, by the first θέμα again, we obtain the schema of the argument διὰ δύο τροπικῶν:

$$\frac{\begin{matrix}1 \supset 2\\ 1 \supset \sim 2\end{matrix}}{\sim 1}$$

But obviously the third θέμα will serve just as well as the θεώρημα in this proof.

[78] The regular way of analyzing was by means of the meta-rules 1–4 (θέματα), but sometimes shorter proofs (presumably making use of previously proved rules) could be found. See *SVF* II, 248.

This argument, according to the Stoics, is compounded out of two type 1 undemonstrated arguments, "as we shall see upon analysis." From (1) and (2), by a type 1 undemonstrated argument, we infer:

> (3) If it is day, it is light.

Now we add (3) to the premises, in accordance with the θεώρημα for the analysis of inferences; and, taking (3) with (2), we infer by another type 1 undemonstrated argument, "Therefore, it is light," which is the conclusion. Thus, says Sextus, the given argument is composed of two type 1 undemonstrated arguments:

> If it is day, then if it is day it is light.
> It is day.
> Therefore, if it is day, it is light.

and

> If it is day, it is light.
> It is day.
> Therefore, it is light.[79]

The second example is the following. Consider the argument-schema:

> (1) If both the first and the second, then the third.
> (2) Not the third.
> (3) The first.
> Therefore, not the second.

Such an argument is compounded of a type 2 and a type 3 undemonstrated argument. From (1) and (2), by a type 2 undemonstrated argument, we get:

> (4) Not both the first and the second,

which, according to the dialectical rule, can now be considered one of the premises, even though it was not explicitly mentioned among them. Next we can construct a type 3 undemonstrated argument from (3) and (4), yielding "Not the second," which was the conclusion. Thus we again have analyzed an argument into two of the basic arguments:

> If both the first and the second, then the third.
> Not the third.
> Therefore, not both the first and the second.

and

---

[79] Sextus, *Adv. Math.* VIII, 230–233.

> Not both the first and the second.
> The first.
> Therefore, not the second.[80]

These, unfortunately, are the only examples we possess of the "innumerable" inferences which the Stoics generated from the five undemonstrated arguments and which made up almost the whole of dialectic.[81] That is to say, these are the only examples for which we possess Stoic proofs. Several other arguments are mentioned or illustrated without proof. For instance, there is the schema:

> Either 1 or 2 or 3.
> Not 1.
> Not 2.
> Therefore 3.

According to Chrysippus, even dogs make use of this sort of argument. For when a dog is chasing some animal and comes to the junction of three roads, if he sniffs first at the two roads down which the animal did not run, he will rush off down the third road without stopping to smell. Chrysippus claimed that the dog *in effect* reasoned as follows:

> Either it went this way or that way or the other way.
> It didn't go this way.
> It didn't go that way.
> Therefore, it went the other way.

It is obvious that this argument, which is said to involve repeated application of the fifth undemonstrated argument, can in fact be analyzed into two applications of that basic argument.[82]

Another inference-schema frequently used by the Stoics was called "the argument from two conditionals" (διὰ δύο τροπικῶν).[83] We are indebted to Origen for preserving the following important Stoic example of this sort of argument:

> If you know that you are dead, you are dead.
> If you know that you are dead, you are not dead.
> Therefore, you do not know that you are dead.

---

[80] *Ibid.*, 234–241.

[81] Cicero, *Topica*, 57.

[82] Sextus, *Hyp. Pyrrh.* I, 69. Another example of this type of argument is to be found at *ibid.*, II, 150. See O. Apelt, "Zu Sextus Empiricus," *Rheinisches Museum*, vol. 39 (1884), pp. 27–28. Unlike Apelt and others who follow him, I take διὰ πλειόνων to mean "repeatedly," i.e., "more than one time." This argument may be analyzed into two applications of the fifth undemonstrated argument-schema, just as the other argument was analyzed by the Stoics into two applications of the first schema.

[83] See the Glossary, s.v. τροπικόν. Łukasiewicz and Stakelum are the only authors who have correctly understood this term; most writers have taken τροπικόν to mean "conditional." I have accepted Stakelum's explanation, as given in *Galen and the Logic of Propositions*, pp. 63–64.

He mentions its Stoic schema:

> If the first, then the second.
> If the first, then not the second.
> Therefore, not the first.[84]

The following is typical of some other arguments used by the Stoics:

> If a sign exists, a sign exists.
> If a sign does not exist, a sign exists.
> Either a sign exists or does not exist.
> Therefore, a sign exists.

The schema was:

> If the first, then the first.
> If not the first, then the first.
> Either the first or not the first.
> Therefore, the first.[85]

No clue is offered on how this sort of argument would be analyzed into the five basic arguments.

In the *Outlines of Pyrrhonism*, Sextus introduces his discussion of the five undemonstrated arguments by saying:

... the "undemonstrated arguments" so much talked of by the Stoics ... are arguments which, they say, need no proof to sustain them *and themselves serve as proofs of the validity of the other arguments* ...

Now they envision many undemonstrated arguments, but the five which they chiefly propound *and to which all the others can, it seems, be referred*, are these: ...[86]

---

[84] Origen, *Contra Celsum* VII, 15 (*Werke*, ed. Koetschau, vol. 2, pp. 166–167). Łukasiewicz ("Zur Geschichte der Aussagenlogik," p. 129, note 29) mentions that Prantl (*Geschichte der Logik im Abendlande*, vol. 1, p. 480) and Zeller (*Die Philosophie der Griechen*, vol. 3, part 1, pp. 114–115, note 5) are proved by Origen's explanation to be in error about the meaning of διὰ δύο τροπικῶν. To these we may add Bury, who says (*Sextus Empiricus*, Loeb Classical Library, vol. 1, p. 151, note *d*): "The hypothetical syllogism 'by two hypotheses' has its major premiss in double form; e.g., 'If *A* is, *B* is, and if *A* is not, *B* is; but *A* either is or is not; therefore *B* is.' "

[85] Sextus, *Adv. Math.* VIII, 281. Cf. *ibid.*, 466, and *Hyp. Pyrrh.* II, 186. The schema occurs at *Adv. Math.* VIII, 292. At *Hyp. Pyrrh.* II, 242, 243, Sextus gives two arguments of which the schema would be:

> If the first, then either the second or the third.
> Not the second.
> Not the third.
> Therefore, not the first.

Such an argument can be analyzed, by means of the first θέμα and Sextus' θεώρημα, into a type 5 and a type 2 undemonstrated argument.

[86] *Hyp. Pyrrh.* II, 156 ff.

The parts of the quotation which I have italicized suggest that the Stoics believed that their propositional logic was complete, in other words, that every valid argument (except arguments containing meta-linguistic terms) could be proved on the basis of arguments of the five undemonstrated types only. Diogenes Laertius mentions this assumption in connection with his account of the undemonstrated arguments:

Also, there are certain "undemonstrated" (because they need no demonstration) arguments, five in number according to Chrysippus (although authorities differ on this), which are used in the construction of every argument. They are assumed in all valid syllogisms, whether categorical or hypothetical.[87]

There are two or three other references to completeness.[88] Evidently some such thesis must have been a part of the Stoic introductions with which Sextus and Diogenes were familiar. Whether Stoic logic was in fact complete cannot be decided until we know all four of the meta-rules for analyzing arguments.

§ 5: INVALID ARGUMENTS; PARADOXES

The Stoic logicians, like logicians of all times, were much interested in the classification and explanation of paradoxes and of invalid arguments. We possess the Stoic classification of invalid arguments and a few of the paradoxes, but most of the great amount of work they did on the latter has been lost.[89]

The principle, if any, which was used by the Stoics in their classification of invalid (ἀσύνακτος or ἀπέραντος)[90] arguments is hard to detect. They distinguished four classes of such arguments, but the classes do not seem to be mutually exclusive:

1. Incoherent arguments (παρὰ διάρτησιν) are arguments which are invalid because there is no logical connection of the premises with one another or with the conclusion.

> If it is day, then it is light.
> Wheat is being sold in the market.
> Therefore, Dion is walking.[91]

---

[87] *Vitae* VII, 79.

[88] *Hyp. Pyrrh.*, II, 166–167, 194; perhaps Cicero, *Topica*, 57, is also a reference to completeness.

[89] See the list of Chrysippus' works given by Diogenes.

[90] At *Hyp. Pyrrh.* II, 146 ff., 152–153, the term ἀσύνακτος is used; in the parallel passages in *Adv. Math.* VIII, 429 ff., the term ἀπέραντος is used. These are synonyms, and there is no reason to translate ἀπέραντος as "indefinite" (as Bury does, *op. cit.*, p. 151, note *d*), since in its logical use περαίνειν meant "to conclude" or "to draw a conclusion." Cf. Epictetus, *Manual*, 44.

[91] *Hyp. Pyrrh.* II, 146; *Adv. Math.* VIII, 430.

2. Redundant arguments (παρὰ παρολκήν) contain a premise which is not necessary for drawing the conclusion.

If it is day, it is light.	If it is day, it is light.
It is day.	It is day.
Dion is walking.	Virtue is beneficial.
Therefore, it is light.	Therefore, it is light.[92]

By all the usual tests these would be perfectly valid arguments, though inelegant. Perhaps Sextus made a mistake here, or perhaps he was following an inferior handbook.

3. Arguments that are propounded in an invalid schema (ἐν μοχθηρῷ σχήματι) are such as the following:

> If it is day, then it is light.
> It is not day.
> Therefore, it is not light.

where the invalid schema is:

> If the first, then the second.
> Not the first.
> Therefore, not the second.[93]

4. Deficient arguments (παρὰ ἔλλειψιν or παρὰ παράλειψιν) contain a premise that is not complete.

> Either wealth is good or wealth is bad.
> It is not bad.
> Therefore, it is good.

This is said to be invalid because of deficiency, since the first premise should be:

> Wealth is either good or bad or neither.[94]

We know also that the Stoics were aware of the vicious-circle fallacy, and had a special name for it (ὁ διάλληλος τρόπος); but we do not possess any discussion of it.[95]

---

[92] *Hyp. Pyrrh.* II, 147; *Adv. Math.* VIII, 431.
[93] *Hyp. Pyrrh.* II, 147–148; *Adv. Math.* VIII, 432–433.
[94] *Hyp. Pyrrh.* II, 150; *Adv. Math.* VIII, 434. Cf. Gellius, *Noctes Atticae* II, vii, 21; V, xi, 8 ff.; XVI, viii, 13.
[95] *Hyp. Pyrrh.* II, 114; *Adv. Math.* VIII, 445. The διάλληλος λόγος was ἀναπόδεικτος as noted in *SVF* II, 273. Compare the ἀδιαφόρως περαίνοντες, p. 66 above.

Much scorn has been heaped upon the Stoics for their interest in paradoxes. In one place Sextus says (of the typical Stoic logician):

> And when he has made a collection of such trash he draws his eyebrows together, and expounds Dialectic and endeavours very solemnly to establish for us by syllogistic proofs that a thing becomes, a thing moves, snow is white, and we do not have horns; although it is probably sufficient to confront the trash with the plain fact in order to smash up their positive affirmation by means of the equipollant contradictory evidence derived from appearances.[96]

The most famous paradox (παράδοξον)[97] considered by the Stoics, and probably the only Stoic paradox which is still of any interest to logicians, is The Liar (ὁ ψευδόμενος). This important antinomy, which allegedly caused at least one fatality in ancient times, was the subject of six books by Chrysippus and also of at least one book by Theophrastus. Chrysippus also wrote many replies to those who thought they could solve it.[98]

The paradox was propounded in several ways. The Apostle Paul, without intending to point out a paradox, reports that Epimenides the Cretan said that all Cretans were liars,[99] and furthermore that what he said was *true*. But The Liar is not stated *as a paradox* in this form by any ancient writer. Typical of the ancient versions is the one reported by Alexander: "The man who says 'I am lying' is both telling the truth and lying."[100] Cicero, after gaining the reader's assent to "If you say that it is now light and tell the truth, then it is now light," proposes "If you say that you are lying and speak the truth, then you are lying."[101] Gellius asks, "When I am lying and say that I am lying, am I not both lying and telling the truth?"[102] It would seem, therefore, that the ancient version of The Liar was a stronger version than the Epimenides. We do not know how any of the competent logicians of antiquity attempted to solve the antinomy. However, Chrysippus wrote books against "those who think that a proposition may be both true and false," and "those who think that the premises of The Liar are false," and "those who solve The Liar by division" (διὰ τῆς τομῆς).[103]

---

[96] *Hyp. Pyrrh.* II, 244 (Bury's trans., Loeb Classical Library, vol. 1, p. 313).

[97] Cicero, *Acad. II*, 136, tells us that παράδοξα was the Stoic term for these puzzles.

[98] Diog. L., *Vitae* V, 49; VII, 196–197. (The victim was Philetas of Cos.) Cf. Seneca, *Ep.*, 45, 10. See also Rüstow, *Der Lügner*.

[99] The paradox is sometimes called "the Epimenides" (Whitehead and Russell, *Principia Mathematica*, vol. 1, p. 60). See Diels (ed. Kranz), *Die Fragmente der Vorsokratiker*, vol. 1, pp. 31–32. While he was at it, Epimenides also called the Cretans "base beasts" and "gluttons": Κρῆτες ἀεὶ ψεῦσται, κακὰ θηρία, γαστέρες ἀργαί.

[100] Alexander, *Ad Soph. El. Comm.*, f65b.

[101] Cicero, *Acad. II*, 96. Of course, this is no antinomy.

[102] Gellius, *Noctes Atticae* XVIII, ii, 10.

[103] Diog. L., *Vitae* VII, 196–197.

The other Stoic paradoxes, though slightly amusing, are too weak to be worth mentioning here.[104]

[104] Thus, "The Horned":

> What you have not lost, you still have.
> You have not lost horns.
> Therefore, you still have horns.

"The Wagon":

> Whatever you say passes through your mouth.
> You say "a wagon."
> Therefore, a wagon passes through your mouth.

"The Nobody":

> If someone is here, then he is not in Rhodes.
> Someone is here.
> Therefore it is not the case that someone is in Rhodes.

For a full discussion of these and other paradoxes, see Prantl, *op. cit.*, pp. 50–58.

CHAPTER VI

EVALUATIONS OF STOIC LOGIC

SUMMARY

IN THIS concluding chapter we consider the traditional evaluations of Stoic logic, together with some of the confusions upon which they are based. The first section concerns some typical adverse criticisms by Prantl and Zeller. Unfortunately, these cannot be challenged by attacking the relevance or accuracy of the evidence for them, since there is no evidence for them. But it is apparent that Prantl and Zeller did not understand Stoic logic. The second section discusses the great confusion which exists in regard to the meaning of the technical term συνημμένον. Third, there is a short conclusion.

§ 1: THE JUDGMENTS OF PRANTL AND ZELLER

Estimates of Stoic logic have not, on the whole, been favorable. In ancient times the Stoics were criticized severely by their many rivals, including the Epicureans, the Skeptics, and especially the Peripatetics. The last were much concerned to defend Aristotelian logic and were apparently the main source of the charges of superficiality often brought against the Stoics.[1] Even Galen, who was fairly well acquainted with Stoic logic, makes repeated accusations that the Stoics paid more attention to the linguistic expressions than to what they meant.[2] The Skeptics, also, did not think highly of Stoic logic. However, although Sextus criticized almost every aspect of Stoic logic, it is clear that he thought that the other logics were even worse. The Epicureans, so far as the writer knows, brought no charges of superficiality against the Stoics; they objected on the grounds that induction rather than deduction was the procedure which ought to be studied.

In modern times the criticism seems to have been based mainly on a general hypothesis to the effect that the Hellenistic age was an age of decline in philosophy. Thus Prantl decided from this point of view that the Stoics were mainly copiers (and poor ones, at that) of the Peripatetic and Megarian doctrines. Accordingly, whenever he found an aspect of the doctrine which he could not understand (which was very often indeed), he put this down as further evidence of miscopying caused by confusion in Stoic minds.

---

[1] Cf. Alexander's many references to this.
[2] On Galen's education, see Galen, *Medicorum Graecorum Opera*, ed. Kuhn, XIX, 43, 47; for the charge against the Stoics, see *Inst. Log.*, p. 11, lines 5 ff.

Prantl disliked Chrysippus with a fervor which, in view of the gap of 2,000 years between them, strikes one as rather odd. He says, "It must have been a frightfully decadent and corrupted age that could designate so hollow a head as Chrysippus as its greatest logician."[3]

Chrysippus created nothing really new in logic, for he only repeated details already known to the Peripatetics or pointed out by the Megarians; his activity consisted in this, that in the treatment of the material he descended to a pitiful degree of dullness, triviality, and scholastic quibbling; or in this, that he created a technical expression for every possible detail, e.g., for the triflings of sophistries and paradoxes;—nomenclature, schematic divisions, establishment of lifeless formal rules—this is the strong side of Chrysippus, and in this, however, he is the man of his times, for he is a prototype of narrow-mindedness and pedantry; it is to be considered a real stroke of luck that the works of Chrysippus were no longer extant in the Middle Ages, for in that extensive morass of formalism, the tendency (weak as it was) toward independent investigation would have been completely eliminated.[4]

What evidence is given for these judgments? The somewhat shocking answer is that his opinions are supported by nothing else than themselves. For instance, when he accuses the Stoics of taking their five undemonstrated argument-schemata from Theophrastus he argues:

However, anyone who stubbornly refuses to believe that these hypothetical inferences actually belonged to the early Peripatetics will certainly be convinced of this by the childish way in which these syllogisms were transformed by the Stoics into the so-called ἀναπόδεικτοι, because clearly that Stoic nonsense must rest on an unintelligent copying of some earlier doctrine, which can be no other than that of the Peripatetics.[5]

The "childish way" (*läppische Weise*) is explained a hundred pages later:

In this connection [i.e., with reference to the five basic undemonstrated argument-types] the boundless stupidity of the Stoics in separating modes IV and V need not be especially emphasized (though mode III is not analyzed into two cases!); indeed Theophrastus also drew a merely formal distinction between these two modes, although in *his* case there was an intelligible reason for so doing. But anybody who merely transcribes the products of other people runs the risk of achieving no more than the exhibition of his own folly.[6]

So far as an argument can be discerned through the rhetoric, it appears to be this: we know that the Stoics were unintelligent copiers because their ἀναπόδεικτοι were silly; our feeling that the ἀναπόδεικτοι were silly is born out by the fact that the Stoics were unintelligent copiers.

---

[3] Prantl, *Geschichte der Logik im Abendlande*, p. 404.

[4] *Ibid.*, p. 408.

[5] *Ibid.*, pp. 379–380. The assertion that Theophrastus discovered the five undemonstrated arguments is based on Philoponus, *In An. Pr.*, 242 ff. But this passage contains no assertion or suggestion that Theophrastus or any of the other early Peripatetics were aware of the five undemonstrated arguments. There is no doubt that post-Chrysippean Peripatetics knew of these arguments.

[6] Prantl, *op. cit.*, pp. 474–475.

Since Prantl offers no real evidence for his critical judgments, we can only evaluate them in a general way by examining the substance and method of his treatment of Stoic logic. He is, unfortunately, confused on almost every major topic. A few examples follow. (1) In pointing out what he considers to be a difficulty in Stoic doctrine, he says, "The word, so far as it expresses a concept of thought, an ἐννόημα, is likewise more than a mere φωνή, that is, it is also a Lekton."[7] But the Stoics never said simply that a word is a Lekton, nor did they ever assert this with any qualifications. Indeed, some of the Stoics thought that there were no such things as Lekta; other Stoics sharply distinguished the Lekta from words; but, so far as we know, none of the Stoics thought that words were Lekta. (2) According to Prantl, "The Stoics divided propositions [ἀξιώματα] into deficient [ἐλλιπῆ] and complete [αὐτοτελῆ]," and in support of this he cites passages in which Sextus and Diogenes say that Lekta are so divided.[8] This indicates that Prantl did not understand the Stoic definition of a proposition (ἀξίωμα) as a "complete Lekton, assertoric in itself." (3) He always translates the Stoic schemata in the following way:

> Wenn das Erste *ist*, so *ist* das Zweite.
> Das Erste aber ja *ist*.
> Also *ist* das Zweite.[9]

This shows that he did not understand that the Stoic variables took propositions as values; no more fundamental confusion about Stoic logic is possible.

Presumably, excellence in method requires both cogency in reasoning and carefulness in investigation. As an example of Prantl's reasoning the following inference will serve: "From the title of one of Plutarch's writings, Περὶ τοῦ πρώτου ἐπομένου πρὸς Χρύσιππον, it may be inferred that there also existed a book Περὶ τοῦ πρώτου ἐπομένου written by Chrysippus himself."[10] As an example of his carelessness, consider the following translation[11] of one of Theophrastus' hypothetical syllogisms δι' ὅλου:

PRANTL	THEOPHRASTUS
Wenn A ist, so ist B.	εἰ τὸ A, τὸ B
Wenn A nicht ist, so ist C.	εἰ οὐ τὸ A, τὸ Γ
Wenn B ist, so ist C nicht.	εἰ οὐ τὸ B, τὸ Γ
oder	ἤ
Wenn C ist, so ist B nicht.	εἰ οὐ τὸ Γ, τὸ B

---

[7] *Ibid.*, p. 421.
[8] *Ibid.*, p. 438. Zeller, *Die Philosophie der Griechen*, vol. 3, part 1, p. 90, note 1, points out this error.
[9] This has been pointed out by Łukasiewicz, "Zur Geschichte . . . ," p. 113.
[10] Prantl, *op. cit.*, p. 408.
[11] *Ibid.*, p. 382.

Zeller's low estimate of Stoic logic may be due in part to the great influence of Prantl. At any rate, Zeller repeats the same general objections (though in much less vehement langage), and his objections are supported by an equally small amount of evidence. His evaluation is contained in the following paragraph:

No very high estimate can therefore be formed of the formal logic of the Stoics. Incomplete as our knowledge of that logic may be, still what is known is enough to determine the judgment absolutely. We see indeed that the greatest care was expended by the Stoics since the time of Chrysippus in tracing the forms of intellectual procedure into their minutest ramifications, and referring them to fixed types. At the same time, we see that the real business of logic was lost sight of in the process, the business of portraying the operations of thought, and giving its laws, whilst the most useless trifling with forms was recklessly indulged in. The Stoics can have made no discoveries of importance even as to logical forms, or they would not have been passed over by writers ever on the alert to note the slightest deviation from the Aristotelian logic. Hence the whole contribution of the Stoics to the field of logic consists in their having clothed the logic of the Peripatetics with a new terminology, and having developed certain parts of it with painful minuteness, whilst they wholly neglected other parts, as was the fate of the part treating of inference. Assuredly it was no improvement for Chrysippus to regard the hypothetical rather than the categorical as the original form of inference. Making every allowance for the extension of the field of logic, in scientific precision it lost more than it gained by the labours of Chrysippus. The history of philosophy cannot pass over in silence this branch of the Stoic system, so carefully cultivated by the Stoics themselves, and so characteristic of their intellectual attitude. Yet, when all has been said, the Stoic logic is only an outpost of their system, and the care which was lavished on it since the time of Chrysippus indicates the decline of intellectual originality.[12]

Again we are unable to scrutinize the evidence for these accusations, because none is given. We are, however, able to examine Zeller's understanding of Stoic logic, and here we find him wanting. His confusion concerning signs and Lekta has been mentioned (chap. ii, note 34). This confusion casts doubt on the trustworthiness of Zeller's judgment that the Stoic semantical theory introduced nothing new and is distinguished from the corresponding Aristotelian theory only by a few changes in expression and a more superficial treatment. We know further that several technical Stoic terms were not understood by Zeller. For example, he explains the technical term συμπεπλεγμένον as "suggesting partly hypothetical sentences like that mentioned in Sextus, *Adv. Math.* VIII, 235, and partly negated categoricals which have the significance of hypotheticals, as: It is not at once A and B."[13] This shows that Zeller could

---

[12] Zeller, *op. cit.*, vol. 3, part 1, p. 117, as translated by Reichel, *Stoics, Epicureans, and Sceptics*, pp. 123–124.

[13] Zeller, *op. cit.*, vol. 3, part 1, p. 111, note 7 (Reichel, p. 117).

not have understood any of the numerous important passages in which the Stoics spoke of conjunctions.

That Zeller would have been equally critical of modern logic is suggested by his criticism of the Stoic διφορούμενοι: "Yet even among these five, importance is attached to some in which the same sentence is repeated tautologically in the form of a conclusion, which proves how mechanical and barren must have been the formalism with which the Stoic logic abounds."[14] He then goes on to comment on the Stoic proof of the schema:

> If the first, then if the first then the second.
> The first.
> Therefore, the second.

He found this proof so strange, so full of useless formalism, that "it is difficult to say exactly what the Stoics intended thereby."[15]

Such remarks as these show that Zeller had little understanding of Stoic logic. Yet he even goes so far as to join Prantl in expressing satisfaction that the Stoic writings were lost.[16] In order to understand this satisfaction, one must remember that scarcity of source material has by no means been inimical to the production of scholarly works in this field.

§ 2: THE CONFUSION ABOUT συνημμένον

It seems probable that confusion about the meaning of the term συνημμένον has done more than any other single factor to obscure the subtleties of Stoic logic. Logicians will appreciate what mayhem would be committed in translating any modern logical treatise if one failed to distinguish between a true conditional proposition and a valid argument. It is therefore no wonder that Stoic logic—which contains such assertions as the following: "An argument is valid if and only if the conditional having the conjunction of the premises as antecedent and the conclusion as consequent is logically true"[17]—has been considered to be merely a collection of empty trivialities. Some examples of the above-mentioned confusion may be instructive.

R. G. Bury, who has made the only English translation of Sextus, says, in a footnote, "Note that the term συνημμένον ('combination') mostly means the 'hypothetical, or major, premiss of a hypothetical syllogism,' but sometimes the whole syllogism."[18] He gives no proof of this; indeed, he could not. The term never means "hypothetical syllo-

[14] *Ibid.*, pp. 113–114 (Reichel, p. 119).
[15] *Ibid.*, p. 114.
[16] *Ibid.*, pp. 115–116.
[17] Sextus, *Adv. Math.* VIII, 417.
[18] Loeb Classical Library, vol. 1, pp. 246–247.

gism," and wherever Bury has so translated, he has corrupted the sense. For example, consider his translation of Sextus, *Adv. Math.* VIII, 415 ff.:

> And they say that the conclusive argument is judged to be conclusive when the conclusion follows from the combination of the premisses; for example, an argument such as this, when it is day—"If it is night, it is dark; but in fact it is night; therefore it is dark"—we declare to be conclusive. . . . For when we have combined the premisses thus, "It is night, and if it is night it is dark," we frame a hypothetical syllogism which begins with this form of combination and ends in this form of conclusion "it is dark." For this hypothetical syllogism is true, as it never begins with truth and ends in falsehood. For when it is day, it will begin with the falsehood "It is night, and if it is night, it is dark," and will end in the falsehood "it is dark," and thus will be true; and in the night, it will both begin with truth and end in truth, and for this very reason it will be true. So, then, the conclusive argument is sound when, after we have combined the premisses and framed a hypothetical syllogism which begins with the combination formed by the premisses and ends in the conclusion, this syllogism itself is found to be true.

A more correct version, in which technical terms are translated by technical terms, would be as follows:

> And they say that the valid argument is judged to be valid when the conclusion is a logical consequent of the conjunction of the premisses; for example, an argument such as this, when it is day—"If it is night, it is dark. But in fact it is night. Therefore it is dark."—we declare to be valid . . . For when we have conjoined the premisses thus, "It is night, and if it is night it is dark," we frame a conditional proposition which has this conjunction as antecedent and the conclusion "it is dark" as consequent. Now this conditional proposition is true since it never has a true antecedent and a false consequent. For when it is day, its antecedent will be the falsehood "It is night, and if it is night, it is dark," and its consequent will be the falsehood "it is dark," and thus it will be true; and in the night, its antecedent and consequent will both be true, and thus it will be true. So, then, an argument is valid whenever, after we have conjoined the premisses and framed the conditional proposition which has the conjunction of the premisses as its antecedent and the conclusion as consequent, it is found that this conditional is true.[19]

In other places where Bury has translated συνημμένον as "hypothetical syllogism" the results have been similar.

For a second example let us consider a recent book by De Lacy. Like Bury, De Lacy gives us a footnote[20] on the term συνημμένον: "This was the basic form of Stoic *inference;* cf. below, 158–160" (italics mine). When we turn to the pages cited, we find a very puzzling account. Commenting on the following statement by Sextus (also mistranslated by Bury): "For a proof is held to be valid whenever its conclusion follows from the conjunction of its premises as a consequent follows an antecedent,"[21] De Lacy says,

---

[19] For the technical items, see the Glossary.
[20] De Lacy, Phillip and Estelle A., *Philodemus: On Methods of Inference*, p. 99. (References to "De Lacy" are intended to include both of the co-authors.)
[21] *Hyp. Pyrrh.* II, 113.

The predominance of the hypothetical proposition in the Stoic scheme indicates their emphasis on the necessary connection between concepts and propositions on the logical level, and between the parts of an interrelated whole on the metaphysical level. The shift in stress from the terms themselves in the categorical propositions and syllogisms of the Aristotelian logic to the relation existing between the terms and propositions expressed by the hypothetical proposition results in the recognition of the relation of necessary consequence, which allows for the inference of one proposition from another.[22]

The connection between the foregoing remarks and the Stoic passage upon which they are based certainly is not clear. Next, De Lacy refers to the different points of view on the truth-conditions of conditionals.[23] Apparently, he does not regard these various points of view as incompatible. But, what is worse, he thinks that the remark of Sextus which was cited sixteen lines above is a statement of one of the proposed criteria for the truth of conditionals.

The definition of a sign as "the proposition in a sound condition which is antecedent and reveals the conclusion" involves first of all an analysis of the conditions for a sound hypothetical proposition. Such a proposition has several criteria. According to the first criterion, the only unsound proposition is one in which the first term is true and the second is false. The Stoic table of sound propositions is as follows:

1. "If it is day, it is light."—sound. The premise is true and the conclusion is true.
2. "If the earth flies, it has wings."—sound. The premise is false and the conclusion is false.
3. "If the earth exists, it flies."—unsound. The premise is true and the conclusion false.
4. "If the earth flies, it exists."—sound. The premise is false and the conclusion true.

The second criterion for a sound condition involves not the literal truth or falsity of the propositions concerned, but the nature of the relation or connection holding between them. The argument is sound when the conclusion follows as a consequence of the "weaving together" (συμπλοκή) or connection of the premises, as in the argument:

> "If it is day, it is light,
> "It is day,
> "Therefore, it is light."[24]

---

[22] De Lacy, *op. cit.*, pp. 158–159. The hypothetical proposition was no more predominant in the Stoic logic than were the disjunctive or conjunctive propositions, if one can judge by the five basic argument-types. Even if it were predominant, this would not indicate emphasis on necessary connection, since Philonian (material) implication had apparently got the upper hand in Stoic logic. But what these remarks have to do with Sextus' principle is not clear. I cite them only to show how completely this ancient version of the deduction theorem has passed over the heads of scholars.

Thus Schmekel, *Forschungen zur Philosophie des Hellenismus*, p. 522, cites a reference to the aforementioned Stoic principle as evidence for his statement: "An inference is only an expanded judgment; the same relation which holds between antecedent and consequent occurs between the premises and conclusion of an inference."

[23] De Lacy, *op. cit.*, p. 159.

[24] *Ibid.*, pp. 159–160. ὑγιές, which he translates as "sound," is synonymous in these

This is the sort of confusion that is generated by confounding arguments with conditionals. It should be observed that Bury and De Lacy have not only misunderstood the Stoics, but also, as a result, have not been able to follow Sextus' own arguments. For example, at *Adv. Math.* VIII, 427–428, Sextus argues that since the Stoics have not agreed upon the truth-conditions for conditionals, and since they say that arguments are valid when and only when the corresponding conditionals are true, the Stoics have not agreed on a criterion for the validity of arguments, either. Neither De Lacy nor Bury shows any evidence of understanding this point.[25]

§ 3: CONCLUSION

There are those who cannot write history without praising and blaming. Such persons, if they are favorably impressed by the newer studies of ancient and medieval logic, will feel that just as Prantl and Zeller praised Aristotelian logic and disparaged that of the Stoics, so now we should praise the Stoic logic and condemn the Aristotelian.

There are also those who cannot write history without embracing certain huge generalizations which are supposed to make history intelligible. This sort of investigator will admit that Prantl, Zeller, and many others have been greatly misled by one such generalization, according to which Hellenistic times were times of decadence and decay in all branches of learning, and especially in philosophy. But he will conclude nothing more than that Prantl, Zeller, and the others have embraced the wrong generalization. In other words, he would propose that we excogitate another (and presumably better) hypothesis about Greco-Roman history and then proceed as before.

Both tendencies are inimical to honest historical writing. There is no reason whatever to believe that an adequate history of logic or of anything else will have the relatively simple structure of a novel. The great generalizations, which are supposed to make the chaos of events intelligible, are, at best, of heuristic value. It must be remembered that they require more evidence than would be required for the support of any of

---

contexts with ἀληθές. συμπλοκή, the technical term for conjunction, should not be translated as "weaving together." There is no virtue in employing etymological translations for technical terms, since a term becomes technical precisely by being *dissociated* from its etymological and other connotations and associated unambiguously with its denotation. Further, the Stoics would never use the terms "premise" and "conclusion" for the parts of a conditional. One wonders, also, to what the phrase *"literal* truth or falsity of the propositions" could possibly refer.

[25] This passage is similar to the one at *Hyp. Pyrrh.* II, 113, which we have been considering; and I assume that if De Lacy cannot understand one, he cannot understand the other. Bury's translations show that he does not follow either passage.

the particular conclusions to be deduced from them. Hence, any conclusion based on such a generalization either can be established without the generalization or else is not warranted at all. But these grand views may well have no heuristic value either, for, as is amply demonstrated by the comments of Prantl and Zeller on Stoic logic, they sometimes have the effect of blinding the scholar to facts which he would otherwise be able to see.

It is difficult to understand how any historian motivated by a desire to discover the truth (rather than by the desire to tell a good story) could share the satisfaction of Prantl and Zeller over the loss of the Stoic writings.

APPENDIX A

THIS APPENDIX consists of translations of some of the fragments which comprise our sources for Stoic logic. I have included only the fragments upon which relatively important sections of this study rest, and, of these, only passages which have not already been adequately translated into English.

SEXTUS EMPIRICUS

The translations have been made from the text of Mutschmann, and all deviations therefrom are noted.

Adv. Math. VIII, 89 ff.

For they [the Stoics] say, "Contradictories are propositions of which the one exceeds the other by a negative," such as "It is day"—"It is not day." For "It is not day" exceeds the proposition "It is day" by the negative "not" and for this reason is its contradictory. But if this is the characteristic of contradictories, such propositions as the following will be contradictory: "It is day and it is light" and "It is day and it is not light." For "It is day and it is not light" exceeds the proposition "It is day and it is light" by a negative. But in fact according to them these are not contradictories. Therefore, propositions do not become contradictory merely through the one exceeding the other by a negative. Yes, they say, but they are contradictories if the following condition is also satisfied: the negative is *prefixed* to the proposition in question, for in that case the negative has scope over[1] the whole proposition; whereas, in the case of "It is day and it is not light," the negative does not have scope enough to negate the whole proposition, since it is inside the proposition. In that case, we will say, it should have been added to the notion of contradictories that they are contradictory not when the one merely exceeds the other by a negative, but when the negative is prefixed to the proposition.

Adv. Math. VIII, 93 ff.

For the Dialecticians proclaim that almost the first and most important distinction among propositions is that according to which some are atomic and some are molecular. Atomic propositions are such as are not compounded from two occurrences of the same proposition or from different propositions[2] by means of one or more connectives, as, for example,

---

[1] In notes 1 to 32, inclusive, the cited page and line numbers refer to Bekker's edition of Sextus (see the inner margin of Mutschmann's edition). 306,26 and 306,28. κυριεύει is translated as "has scope over" or "governs." See the Glossary.

[2] 307,25. Kochalsky's addition ⟨καί⟩ probably should be left out, for it certainly does not improve the sense. There is no doubt that διὰ τινὸς ἢ τινῶν συνδέσμων modifies the verb and does not merely go with *one* of the clauses. The statement means, "Atomic propositions are such as are not compounded by means of connectives from two occurrences of the same proposition or from different propositions." The statement at 308,6 ff., which is collated by Kochalsky, means merely, "and molecular

[95]

"It is day," "It is night," "Socrates is conversing," and every proposition of similar form ... For example, "It is day" is atomic so far as it is neither composed of two occurrences of the same proposition nor of different propositions, although, of course, it is put together out of certain other elements, namely, "day" and "it is." Moreover, there is no connective in it, either. But molecular propositions are such as are, as it were, "double," and are composed from two occurrences of the same proposition or from different propositions, and are composed by means of a connective or connectives. For example, "If it is day, it is day" ... "It is day and it is light," "It is day or it is night."

Adv. Math. VIII, 96 ff.

Of atomic propositions, some are definite, some are indefinite, and some are intermediate. Definite propositions are those which are deictically expressed. For example, "This [man] is walking," "This [man] is sitting" (I am pointing at some particular person). Indefinite propositions, according to them, are those over which some indefinite particle has scope. For example, "Someone is sitting." And intermediate propositions are those like "A man is sitting" or "Socrates is walking." Now "Someone is walking" is an indefinite proposition because it does not determine any particular walking person, for it may be asserted with reference to *any* such person; but "This [man] is sitting" is definite because it determines the person whom the speaker indicates. And "Socrates is sitting down" is an intermediate proposition, for it is neither indefinite (since it determines the species) nor definite (since it is not asserted deictically), but seems rather to be intermediate between the definite and the indefinite. And they say that the indefinite proposition—"Someone is walking" or "someone is sitting"—is true whenever the definite proposition—"This man is walking" or "This man is sitting"—is found to be true; for if no particular person is sitting, the indefinite proposition "Someone is sitting" cannot be true ... and they say that this definite proposition is true when and only when the subject pointed out has the predicate in question, that is, "sitting" or "walking."

Adv. Math. VIII, 108 ff.

And now that we have to some extent handled the rules of the Dialecticians in the case of atomic propositions, let us proceed also to those

---

propositions are such as are compounded from the same or different propositions and [compounded] by means of a connective or connectives." Any suggestion that molecular sentences might be compounded by some other means than the connectives is in part refuted by the examples which are given. Cf. 311,17 ff.

which concern the molecular. Molecular propositions are those already mentioned above, that is, such as are composed of differing propositions or of two occurrences of the same proposition and[3] contain a connective or connectives. Of these, let us take for the present the so-called "conditional." This, then, is composed of a duplicated proposition or of differing propositions[4] by means of the connective "if."[5] Thus, for example, from a duplicated proposition by the connective "if" there is composed such a conditional as "If it is day, it is day"; and from differing propositions by means of the connective "if" [εἴπερ] there is composed one like this: "If [εἴπερ] it is day, it is light." Of the propositions in the conditional, the one that immediately follows the connective "if"[6] is called "the antecedent" and "the first," and the other one is called "the consequent" and "the second," even if the whole conditional is asserted in reverse order, as, for example, "It is light if [εἴπερ] it is day"; for in this, too, "It is light" is called "the consequent" even though it was said first, and "It is day" is called "the antecedent," even though it was said second, because it comes directly after the connective "if" [εἴπερ].

Such, to put it briefly, is the construction of the conditional. Such a proposition seems to announce that the second part of it follows from the first: that is, if the antecedent holds, so will the consequent.[7] Hence, if this sort of announcement is fulfilled, that is, if the consequent does follow from the antecedent, then the conditional is true; otherwise it is false.

Adv. Math. VIII, 112 ff.

Now all the Dialecticians agree in asserting that a conditional holds whenever its consequent follows from its antecedent; but as to when and how it follows, they disagree with one another and set forth conflicting criteria for this "following." For example, Philo said that the conditional is true whenever it is not the case that its antecedent is true and its consequent false; so that, according to him, the conditional is true in three cases and false in one case. For it is true whenever the antecedent is true and the consequent is true. For example, "If it is day, it is light." Again, it is true whenever the antecedent is false and the consequent is false. For example, "If the earth flies, then the earth has wings." It is also true whenever the antecedent is false and the consequent is true.

[3] 311,17 ff. See note 2.
[4] 311,21. Kochalsky's addition of καί serves no purpose. See note 2.
[5] 311,21. "If" seems to be the best translation for both εἰ and εἴπερ.
[6] See note 5.
[7] 312,5. I have here supposed that when Sextus said "is" he meant "is true" or "holds." The metaphysical question whether or not propositions exist does not seem to be involved in this passage.

For example, "If the earth flies, then the earth exists." It is false only when the antecedent is true and the consequent is false, as, for example, "If it is day, then it is night." For when it is day the antecedent, "It is day," is true, and the consequent, "It is night," is false.

But Diodorus says that a conditional is true whenever it neither ever was nor is possible for the antecedent to be true and the consequent false, which is incompatible with Philo's thesis. For, according to Philo, such a conditional as "If it is day, then I am conversing" is true when it is day and I am conversing, since in that case its antecedent, "It is day," is true and its consequent, "I am conversing," is true; but according to Diodorus it is false. For it is possible for its antecedent, "It is day," to be true and its consequent, "I am conversing," to be false at some time, namely, after I have become quiet. And it was possible for its antecedent to be true and its consequent false, for before I began to converse, the antecedent, "It is day," was true, but the consequent, "I am conversing," was false. Again, according to Philo, a proposition like "If it is night, then I am conversing" is true when it is day and I am silent, since the antecedent is false and the consequent is false; but according to Diodorus such a proposition is false. For it is possible that its antecedent be true and its consequent false (when night has come on and I am not conversing). Moreover, according to Philo, "If it is night, then it is day" is true when it is day, because its antecedent, "It is night," is false, whereas its consequent, "It is day," is true; but according to Diodorus the proposition is false, since it is possible (when night has come on) for its antecedent, "It is night," to be true, while its consequent, "It is day," is false.

Adv. Math. VIII, 125.

. . . they say that a conjunction holds when all the conjuncts are true, but is false when it has at least one false conjunct . . . they say that, just as in daily life we do not say that a cloak is sound [holds] just because most of it is sound and only a small part is torn, but on the contrary we say that it is torn because of the small part that is torn, so also in the case of a conjunction that has one false conjunct and several true ones, the whole will be said to be false because of the one false part.

Adv. Math. VIII, 215 ff.

Aenesidemus, in the fourth book of the Pyrrhonean Discourses, argues for the same hypothesis and with about the same force, as follows: "If phenomena appear in like manner to all those who are in a similar condition and signs are phenomena, then signs appear in like manner to all those who are in a similar condition. Signs do not appear in like manner to all those who are in a similar condition. Phenomena do appear in like manner to all those who are in a similar condition. Therefore, signs are not phenomena." Here Aenesidemus appears to use the term "phenomena" to mean perceptibles, and he argues an argument in which a second undemonstrated argument is superimposed upon a third; its schema is:

> If both the first and the second, then the third.
> Not the third.
> The first.
> Therefore, not the second.

We shall show a little later that in fact this is so. But now we shall simply prove that the premises are true and that the conclusion follows from them. In the first place, therefore, the conditional is true. For its consequent, which is "Signs appear in like manner to all those who are in a similar condition," follows from the conjunction, which is "Phenomena appear in like manner to all those who are in a similar condition and signs are phenomena" . . . So the conditional is true. True also is the second premise, namely, "Signs do not appear in like manner to all those who are in a similar condition" . . . Thus the second premise is also true. But so is the third: "Phenomena appear in like manner to all those who are in a similar condition" . . . Therefore the conclusion, "Signs are not phenomena," will have been inferred from true premises.

Thus, in the first place, the argument has been shown by our investigation to be true. That it is also undemonstrated and syllogistic will appear when we analyze it.

Adv. Math. VIII, 223.

For—to go back a little way—the term "undemonstrated," to start with, has two senses, being used both of arguments which have not been demonstrated and of those which have no need of demonstration owing to the fact that it is at once obvious that they are valid. And we have many times indicated that the arguments at the beginning of Chrysippus' "First Introduction to Syllogisms" are given this title in the second sense. Thus now, in accordance with this, one must understand that a type 1 undemonstrated argument is that which is made up of a conditional and its antecedent, and which has the consequent of the conditional for a conclusion. That is, when an argument has two premises, of which one is a conditional and the other is the antecedent of the conditional, and also has as its conclusion the consequent of the same conditional, then such an argument is said to be an instance of a type 1 undemonstrated argument, for example, such an argument as this:

> If it is day, then it is light.
> It is day.
> Therefore, it is light.

For this has a conditional as one of its premises:

> If it is day, then it is light.

And for the other premise it has the antecedent of the conditional:

> It is day.

And third, for its conclusion it has the consequent of the conditional:

> It is light.

A type 2 undemonstrated argument is that which is made up of a conditional and the denial of its consequent, and which has the contradictory of the antecedent for a conclusion. That is, when an argument has two premises, of which the one is a conditional and the other is the contradictory of the consequent of the conditional, and also has as its conclusion the contradictory of the antecedent, then such an argument is an instance of a type 2 undemonstrated argument. For example:

> If it is day, then it is light.
> It is not light.
> Therefore, it is not day.

For "If it is day, then it is light," which is one of the premises, is a conditional, and "It is not light," which is the other premise, is the contradictory of the consequent of the conditional; and the conclusion, "It is not day," is the contradictory of the antecedent. A type 3 undemonstrated argument is one made up of a negated conjunction and one of the conjuncts, and which has as its conclusion the contradictory of the other conjunct. For example:

> Not both: it is day and it is night.
> It is day.
> Therefore, it is not night.

For "Not both: it is day and it is night" is the negation of the conjunction "It is day and it is night," and "It is day" is one of the conjuncts, while "It is not night" is the contradictory of the other member of the conjunction.

Such then are the arguments. The "moods" or "schemata" in which such arguments are given follow.

For a type 1 undemonstrated argument:

> If the first, then the second
> The first.
> Therefore, the second.

For a type 2 undemonstrated argument:

> If the first, then the second.
> Not the second.
> Therefore, not the first.

For a type 3 argument:

> Not both the first and the second.
> The first.
> Therefore, not the second.

It is further necessary to recognize that of the undemonstrated arguments some are simple, others not simple. Simple arguments are those such that it is immediately clear that they are valid, that is, their conclusion validly follows from their premises.[8] The arguments stated above are of this kind, for, in the case of the first type, if we grant that "If it is day, then it is light" is true (I mean that its being light follows from its being day) and if we assume the first ("It is day"), which is the antecedent of the conditional, it will necessarily follow that it is also light, which was the conclusion of the argument. Not simple are those which are compounded of simple ones and which further must be analyzed into the simples if we are to know that they are valid. Of these not-simple arguments, some are made up of homogeneous parts and some of heterogeneous: of homogeneous, as in arguments compounded from two type 1 or type 2 undemonstrated arguments; of heterogeneous, as in arguments consisting of a type 1 and a type 3[9] undemonstrated argument, or

---

[8] 337,6. I have translated συνεισάγω as if it were synonymous with συνάγω. However, συνεισάγω seems to be used only in examples in which the validity of the argument is immediately clear.

[9] 337,19. Here I follow Kochalsky's (83) suggestion of καὶ τρίτον for the lacuna, although, as Mutschmann notes, καὶ δευτέρου is equally possible. The first mentioned could have been illustrated by such an argument as:

$$p \supset (q \supset r)$$
$$p$$
$$\sim r$$
$$\overline{\sim q}$$

of a type 2 and a type 3 argument, and suchlike. Thus an argument such as the following is composed of homogeneous parts:

> If it is day, then if it is day it is light.[10]
> It is day.
> Therefore, it is light.

For it is made out of two type 1 undemonstrated arguments, as we shall see upon analysis. One should observe that there is a dialectical theorem handed down for the analysis of syllogisms, namely, "Whenever we have premises which yield a conclusion, we have in effect also this conclusion among the premises, even if it is not explicitly stated." Since, therefore, we have two premises, namely, (1) the conditional "(If it is day, then) if it is day then it is light,"[11] the antecedent of which is the atomic proposition "It is day," and the consequent of which is the molecular conditional, "If it is day, then it is light," and (2) the antecedent, "It is day," of the main conditional, from these we shall infer, by a type 1 undemonstrated argument, the main conditional's consequent: "If it is day, then it is light." In effect, therefore, we have in the argument this inferred proposition, although it is left out of the explicit statement. Putting it beside[12] the premise "It is day" of the main argument, we infer by a type 1 undemonstrated argument, "It is light," which was the con-

---

and the second by this:

$$p \supset \sim(q.r)$$
$$p$$
$$q$$
$$\overline{}$$
$$\sim r$$

Fabricius, whom Bekker follows, took the words καὶ τρίτου to go not only with ἐκ δευτέρου but also with ἐκ πρώτου ἀναποδείκτου; but I would agree with Kochalsky that this violates normal usage.

[10] 337,22. Kochalsky's addition of εἰ ἡμέρα ἐστίν is required for the sense. Rüstow's addition makes nonsense of the argument, and the text as it stands also makes nonsense of the argument. To illustrate a nonsimple homogeneous argument, Sextus here offers:

> (1) If it is day, then if it is day it is light.
> (2) It is day.
>   Therefore, it is light.

For further explanation see p. 63 above.

[11] 337,30. Kochalsky's addition of εἰ ἡμέρα ἐστίν, φῶς ἐστιν is required for the sense. As the text stands, with the addition which Mutschmann adopts from Fabricius, it reads, "the conditional 'If it is day, then it is light,' whose antececent is the atomic proposition 'It is day' and whose consequent is the molecular conditional 'If it is day, then it is light,' " which is of course incorrect.

[12] 338,6. Kochalsky's addition of δ brings this passage into line with the general dialectical theorem mentioned above, to which it plainly refers. See note 2.

clusion of the main argument. So there are two type 1 undemonstrated arguments, one of which runs:

> If it is day, then if it is day it is light.
> It is day.
> Therefore, if it is day, it is light.[13]

and one of which runs:

> If it is day, then it is light.
> It is day.
> Therefore, it is light.

Such, then, is the character of arguments constructed of homogeneous parts. Next come those with heterogeneous parts, such as that which was propounded by Aenesidemus concerning The Sign and which goes as follows: "If phenomena appear in like manner to all those who are in a similar condition and signs are phenomena, then signs appear in like manner to all those who are in a similar condition. Signs do not appear in like manner to all those who are in a similar condition. Phenomena appear in like manner to all those who are in a similar condition. Therefore, signs are not phenomena." Such an argument is composed of a type 2 undemonstrated argument and a type 3 undemonstrated argument, as may be learned from the analysis, which will be clearer when we have given the schema:

> If both the first and the second, then the third.
> Not the third.
> The first.
> Therefore, not the second.

For, since we have a conditional in which the antecedent is a conjunction, "the first and the second," and in which the consequent is "the third," and we have further the contradictory ("not the third") of the consequent, we shall infer by a type 2 argument the contradictory of the antecedent, "not both the first and the second." But this very conclusion is in effect contained in the argument, since we have the premises which yield it, though it is not stated explicitly. Putting this[14] beside the remaining premise, "the first," we infer the conclusion, "Therefore, not the

---

[13] 338,10 ff. Again, Kochalsky's additions are necessary to preserve sense. Rüstow's additions and Mutschmann's text are equally hopeless.

[14] 339,4. ὅπερ is needed, instead of ἄπερ, since it is the single proposition "not both the first and the second" that we put beside the remaining premise. We do *not* put the two premises just used beside the remaining premise, as ἄπερ suggests. See note 12. Heintz (173) and Kochalsky (85) read ὅπερ.

second," by a type 3 undemonstrated argument. So there are two undemonstrated arguments, one which runs:

> If both the first and the second, then the third.
> Not the third.
> Therefore, not both the first and the second.

which is a type 2 argument; and the other, a type 3 argument, which
runs:

> Not both the first and the second.
> The first.
> Therefore, not the second.

Such, then, is the analysis in the case of the schema, and in the case
of the argument it is analogous; for the third premise is left out, namely,
"Not both: Phenomena appear in like manner to all those who are in a
similar condition, and signs are phenomena," which, together with "Phenomena appear in like manner to all those in a similar condition,"
yields the conclusion[15] of the main argument by a type 3 undemonstrated
argument. So our analysis yields a type 2 argument: "If phenomena
appear in like manner to all those in a similar condition, and signs are
phenomena, then signs appear in like manner to all those in a similar
condition. But signs do not appear in like manner to all those in a similar
condition. Therefore not both: Phenomena appear in like manner to all
those who are in a similar condition, and signs are phenomena";[16] and a
type 3 argument like this: "Not both: Phenomena appear in like manner
to all those in a similar condition, and signs are phenomena. But phenomena appear in like manner to all those in a similar condition. Therefore, signs are not phenomena."

---

[15] 339,17. I have supposed that this lacuna should be filled with λόγου συμπέρασμα,
at least. See Kochalsky (85).

[16] 339,23. After φαίνεται we should have, as Kochalsky (86) proposes,

οὐκ ἄρα καὶ τὰ φαινόμενα πᾶσ. τοῖς ὁμοίως διακειμένοις παραπλησίως φαίνεται
καὶ τὰ σημεῖά ἐστι φαινόμενα

instead of

τὰ σημεῖα ἄρα οὐκ ἔστι φαινόμενα

which appears in Mutschmann's text and is accepted by Bury, because the conclusion
of this argument must be the first premise of the next argument and must therefore
be the same as what appears in lines 24–26. It must also be the denial of the antecedent of the conditional which appears in lines 19–22. There is therefore no doubt that,
unless Sextus himself made an error here, the text should be emended as shown
above. Heintz (174) prefers the assumption that Sextus made an error to the assumption that the text is corrupt. Mutschmann's version of Kochalsky's emendation would
give, "Therefore the phenomena do not appear in like manner to all those in a similar
condition and therefore signs are not phenomena." This cannot be validly inferred
from the premises given, nor would it serve as a premise in the succeeding argument.

Adv. Math. VIII, 245 ff.

They say that there are many other tests for a true conditional but that there is one test, about to be described, which, though even *it* is not agreed upon, is superior to all. Every conditional has either a true antecedent and a true consequent, or a false antecedent and a false consequent, or a true and a false, or a false and a true. "If there are gods, then the universe is conducted according to divine foresight" has a true antecedent and a true consequent. "If the earth is flying, then the earth has wings" has a false antecedent and a false consequent. "If the earth is flying, then the earth exists" has a false antecedent and a true consequent. "If he is moving, then he is walking" has a true antecedent and a false consequent, provided he is not walking but is moving. Since, then, there are four possible combinations for the parts of a conditional—true antecedent and true consequent, false antecedent and false consequent, false and true, or conversely true and false—they say that in the first three cases the conditional is true (i.e., if the antecedent is true and the consequent is true, it is true; if false and false, it again is true; likewise, for false and true); but in one case only is it false, namely, whenever the antecedent is true and the consequent is false.

Adv. Math. VIII, 281 ff.

Some also argue thus:

> If a sign exists, then a sign exists.
> If a sign does not exist, then a sign exists.
> Either a sign exists or does not exist.
> Therefore, it exists.

Such is the argument; and they say that its first premise holds, for it is repeated, and "A sign exists" follows from "A sign exists," since, if the first is true, so is the second (which is no different from the first). They say also that "If a sign does not exist, a sign exists" holds; for stating that a sign does not exist involves stating that there is a sign. For if no sign exists, there will be some sign that no sign exists . . . So the first two premises are, they say, true. And the third is also true. For it is a disjunction of the contradictories "A sign exists" and "A sign does not exist." For if every disjunction is true when and only when it has one true disjunct, and if of contradictories one is always considered true, one must say without reservation that a premise so constructed is true. So the conclusion, too, "A sign exists," is inferred on the basis of the agreed premises.

It will also be possible, they say, to examine the argument thus: there are in the argument two conditionals and one disjunction; of these, the conditionals announce that their consequents follow from their antecedents, and the disjunction has one of its disjuncts true, since if both are true or both false the whole will be false. Such being the force of the premises, let us assume that one of the disjuncts is true and see how the conclusion is inferred. First, let "A sign exists" be assumed as true; then, since this is the antecedent in the first conditional, we will get, following from it, the consequent of that conditional. That consequent was "A sign exists," which is the same as the conclusion. The conclusion will have been inferred, therefore, under the assumption that "A sign exists" is true. On the other hand, let us assume the other disjunct, "A sign does not exist," to be true. Since this is the antecedent of the second conditional, we will get, as following from it, the consequent of the second conditional. But what followed from it was "A sign exists," which is also the conclusion. Therefore, in this way too the conclusion is deduced.

Adv. Math. VIII, 332.

Let us state at once that a conditional holds unless its antecedent is true and its consequent is false.

Adv. Math. VIII, 415 ff.

And they say that the criterion for validity is that an argument is valid whenever the conclusion follows logically from the conjunction of the premises. For example, such an argument (when it is day) as the following is said to be valid (though not true,[17] since its conclusion is false):

> If it is night, it is dark.
> It is night.
> Therefore, it is dark.

For conjoining the premises thus,

> It is night and if it is night it is dark.

we form a conditional having this conjunction as its antecedent and the conclusion "It is dark" as its consequent. But this conditional is true, since it never has a true antecedent and a false consequent. For when it is day, the antecedent, "It is night and if it is night it is dark," is false, and its consequent, "It is dark," is false, and so the conditional is true.

---

[17] 377,16. Note that the definition of "truth" as applied to propositions is very different from the definition of "truth" as applied to arguments; in fact, the definiens of the definition of "truth" in the latter sense contains "truth" in its former sense. See 377,32 ff. See the Glossary, s.v. ἀληθής.

And at night it will have a true antecedent and a true consequent and will therefore also be true. So, then, an argument is really valid when, after we have conjoined the premises and formed the conditional having the conjunction of the premises as antecedent and the conclusion as consequent, it is found that this conditional is true. And that an argument is true is decided not solely from the fact that the conditional which has the conjunction of the premises as its antecedent and the conclusion as its consequent is true, but also from whether or not the conjunction formed from the premises is true,[18] since if one of these is found to be false the argument will necessarily become false; so the following (when it is night):

> If it is day, it is light.
> It is day.
> Therefore, it is light.

is judged to be false because it has the false premise "It is day." However, the conjunction of the premises, having one false conjunct ("It is day"), is false; but the conditional having the conjunction of the premises as its antecedent and the conclusion as its consequent will be true. For it never has a true antecedent and a false consequent, but when it is night the antecedent conjunction is false, and when it is day the consequent as well as the antecedent is true. But such an argument as this is false:[19]

> If it is day, it is light.
> It is light.
> Therefore, it is day.

for it allows us to infer a false conclusion from true premises. But if we test it we find it is possible for the conjunction of the premises, "It is light and if it is day it is light," to be true (when it is light), but the conditional having the conjunction of the premises as its antecedent and the conclusion as its consequent to be false,[20] thus, "If (it is light and if it is day it is light)[21] then it is day." For this conditional can, when it is night,

---

[18] ὑγιές. See the Glossary.

[19] 378,17 ff. He has just finished giving an example of an argument that is false though valid. Now he offers an example of an argument that is false because it is invalid. An argument is false if either it is invalid or it has a false conclusion (or both). Cf. 88.

[20] 378,23. Heintz (196) thinks that ἔστιν should be added after ψεῦδος in line 23 and that, correspondingly, ἔσται should replace εἶναι in line 27. Basing his considerations on Diodorus' definition of implication, he argues that when it is possible for the antecedent to be true and the consequent false, the conditional is not merely *possibly* false; rather, it *is* false.

[21] 378,24. ἡμέρα ἐστιν must be added after φῶς ἐστιν, as Kochalsky (92) and Heintz (197) say, and as Mutschmann failed to observe. See my article, "Stoic Logic . . .," in connection with this and the other similar emendations mentioned in notes 26, 28, and 30.

have a true conjunction for its antecedent, but a false consequent, "It is day," and can therefore be false. So an argument is "true" neither when the conjunction only, nor when the conditional only, is true, but only when both are true.

Adv. Math. VIII, 426.

. . . they say that an argument is valid whenever there is a true conditional which has the conjunction of the premises as its antecedent and the conclusion as its consequent . . .

Adv. Math. VIII, 466 ff.

And some, too, argue thus:

> If proof exists, then proof exists.
> If proof does not exist, then proof exists.
> Either proof exists or proof does not exist.
> Therefore, proof exists.

And the convincing character of the premises of this argument is clear. For the first conditional, "If proof exists, proof exists," constituting a duplication, is true. For its consequent follows from its antecedent, since it is not different. The second conditional, "If proof does not exist, proof exists," again, holds. For the existence of proof follows from the non-existence of proof, which is its antecedent; for the very argument which shows the nonexistence of proof certifies, because it is demonstrative, that there is proof. The disjunction, "Either proof exists or proof does not exist," formed from the contradictory disjuncts, "Proof exists" and "Proof does not exist," must[22] have one true disjunct and therefore must be true. Thus, since the premises are true, the conclusion is proved. It is possible to show in another way that the conclusion follows from the premises. Since the disjunction is true if one of its disjuncts is true, whichever one of these we assume to be true, the conclusion will be inferred.[23] Let the first disjunct, "Proof exists," be assumed as true. Since this is the antecedent of the first conditional, the consequent of the first conditional will follow from it. But that was "Proof exists," which was the conclusion. So, granting the truth of the disjunct, "Proof exists," the conclusion of the argument will follow. And the same manner of argumentation applies also to the remaining proposition, "Proof does not

[22] 388,24. The Greek word here translated as "must" is ὀφείλει.
[23] See note 8.

exist"; for this is the antecedent of the second conditional and[24] it had as a consequence the conclusion of the argument.

Hyp. Pyrrh. II, 104 ff.

. . . the Stoics, in attempting to establish the conception of the sign, say that a sign is a proposition which is the antecedent of a true conditional and which is indicative of the consequent. And they say that a proposition is a complete Lekton which is assertoric in itself, and that a true conditional is one which does not have a true antecedent and a false consequent. For the conditional either has a true antecedent and a true consequent, as, "If it is day, it is light"; or it has a false antecedent and a false consequent, such as, "If the earth flies, the earth is winged"; or it has a true antecedent and a false consequent, as, "If the earth exists, then the earth flies"; or it has a false antecedent and a true consequent, such as, "If the earth flies, then the earth exists." Of these, only the one having a true antecedent and a false consequent fails to hold, according to them, and the others hold.

Hyp. Pyrrh. II, 110 ff.

For Philo says that a true conditional is one which does not have a true antecedent and a false consequent; for example, when it is day and I am conversing, "If it is day, then I am conversing"; but Diodorus defines it as one which neither is nor ever was capable of having a true antecedent and a false consequent. According to him, the conditional just mentioned seems to be false, since when it is day and I have become silent, it will have a true antecedent and a false consequent; but the following conditional seems true: "If atomic elements of things do not exist, then atomic elements of things do exist," since it will always have the false antecedent, "Atomic elements of things do not exist," and the true consequent, "Atomic elements of things do exist." And those who introduce connection or coherence say that a conditional holds whenever the denial of its consequent is incompatible with its antecedent; so, according to them, the above-mentioned conditionals do not hold, but the following is true: "If it is day, then it is day." And those who judge by "suggestion"[25] declare that a conditional is true if its consequent is in effect included in its antecedent. According to these, "If it is day, then it is day," and every repeated conditional will probably be false, for it is impossible for a thing itself to be included in itself.

---

[24] 389,5. The "and" is added by Kochalsky to fill a lacuna in the text.
[25] 82,14. ἔμφασις, the "power of signifying more than is explicitly expressed" (Bury).

Hyp. Pyrrh. II, 113.

For a proof is held to be valid whenever its conclusion follows from the conjunction of its premises as a consequent follows from an antecedent, such as [for]:

> If it is day, then it is light.
> It is day.
> Therefore, it is light.

[we have] "If (if it is day then it is light, and it is day) then it is light."[26]

Hyp. Pyrrh. II, 135 ff.

A proof, as they say, is an argument which, by means of agreed premises, leads logically to a nonevident conclusion. What they mean will become more clear from the following. An argument is a system consisting of premises and a conclusion. Those propositions which are agreed upon for the establishment of the conclusion are called "premises," and the proposition which is established from the premises is called the "conclusion," as, for instance, in the following argument:

> If it is day, then it is light.
> It is day.
> Therefore, it is light.

The proposition "It is light" is the conclusion and the others are premises. Some arguments are valid and some are not valid: valid, whenever the conditional whose antecedent is the conjunction of the premises and whose consequent is the conclusion, is true. For instance, the previously mentioned argument is valid, since "It is light" follows from the premise-conjunction, "It is day and if it is day it is light,"[27] in this conditional: "If (it is day and if it is day it is light) then it is light."[28] Arguments not like these are invalid.

---

[26] 82,25–26. Instead of

> εἴπερ ἡμέρα ἐστιν . . .

we should have

> εἴπερ εἰ ἡμέρα ἐστί, φῶς ἐστι καὶ ἡμέρα ἐστὶ φῶς ἐστιν

which Heintz would call a "monstrosity" (see pp. 62–63, 195), but which, as he says, makes good sense in this context. We merely add an εἰ and drop a καί; or the καί may be left in and read as "also." Mutschmann's use of quotation marks here is confusing. The argument is given first and is followed by the corresponding conditional. Cf. Heintz (51). Usually the antecedent of such a conditional is commuted, but this is more exactly what is described.

[27] 88,5–6. Mutschmann's quotation marks are in the wrong places: ἡμέρα ἐστὶ καὶ εἰ ἡμέρα ἐστὶ φῶς ἐστιν is one statement and should be quoted as a unit.

[28] 88,7. The text as given by Mutschmann is unintelligible. Nor does Rüstow's

Of the valid arguments, some are true and some are not true: true, whenever not only is there a true conditional consisting of the premise-conjunction and the conclusion, as we said before, but also[29] the premise-conjunction, which is the antecedent in the conditional, is true. And a conjunction like "It is day and if it is day it is light" is true whenever every conjunct is true. Arguments not having the above-described characteristic are not true. For such an argument as the following is valid:

> If it is night, it is dark.
> It is night.
> Therefore, it is dark.

since the following conditional holds: "If (it is night and if it is night it is dark) then it is dark,"[30] but the argument is not true. For the conjunctive antecedent is false, since it contains the false conjunct "It is night";[31] for a conjunction containing a false conjunct is false. Hence they also say that a true argument is one which leads logically from true premises to a true conclusion.

Hyp. Pyrrh. II, 156 ff.

. . . the undemonstrated arguments so much talked of by the Stoics . . . are arguments which, they say, need no proof to sustain them and themselves serve as proofs of the conclusiveness of the other arguments . . .[32]

---

removal of εἰ help at all. Since we have been told what the parts of the conditional are, no great skill is required to reconstruct it. Following Sextus' instructions, we get

εἰ (ἡμέρα ἐστί, καὶ εἰ ἡμέρα ἐστί, φῶς ἐστι) φῶς ἐστιν

instead of

εἰ ἡμέρα ἐστί, καὶ εἰ ἡμέρα ἐστί, φῶς ἐστιν

where the parentheses show how it is to be understood. Heintz (62) agrees with Pappenheim's version, which ends with φῶς ἄρα ἐστίν and is otherwise the same as that proposed above. It is clear, however, that ἄρα is the sign of the conclusion of an argument and has no place in a conditional. The sharp distinction between an argument and its corresponding conditional is often overlooked by the editors, but never by the Stoics. See note 30.

[29] 88,11–12. καὶ τὸ συμπέρασμα should be taken out. This raises the question of what to do with αὐτοῦ. Cf. Heintz (65). Either it may be taken out or it may be regarded as referring to an unmentioned antecedent, λόγος. The parallel passage at 378,3 seems to suggest the latter course. A third possibility, mentioned by Heintz (65), but hardly credible, is that αὐτοῦ refers to τὸ συμπέρασμα, and that this passage is nonsense.

[30] 88,19–20. This should be reconstructed in accordance with the context to read

εἰ νύξ ἐστι, καὶ εἰ νύξ ἐστι, σκότος ἐστί, σκότος ἐστίν

The ἄρα in line 20 must go, since a conditional (συνημμένον) is defined to be a *proposition*, not an argument. See note 28 and Heintz (62).

[31] We are apparently proceeding under the assumption that it is day. See Bury's translation of this passage.

[32] 92,26. Mutschmann's addition of διά is worse than unnecessary. Compare 92,30 and the corresponding passage in Diog. L., *Vitae* VII, 79. As Heintz points out (66–67), Mutschmann's addition tends to reverse the sense of the passage, which is an assertion about the completeness of Stoic propositional logic. Cf. also 95,11 ff. and 102,8–10.

Now they envision many undemonstrated arguments, but the five which they chiefly propound and to which all the others can, it seems, be referred, are these. From a conditional and its antecedent, the first yields the consequent. For example:

> If it is day, then it is light.
> It is day.
> Therefore, it is light.

From a conditional and the contradictory of its consequent, the second yields the contradictory of the antecedent. For example:

> If it is day, then it is light.
> It is not light.
> Therefore, it is not day.

From the denial of a conjunction and one of the conjuncts, the third yields the contradictory of the other conjunct. For example:

> Not both it is day and it is light.
> It is day.
> Therefore, it is not light.

From a disjunction and one of the disjuncts, the fourth yields the contradictory of the other disjunct. For example:

> Either it is day or it is night.
> It is day.
> Therefore, it is not night.

From a disjunction and the contradictory of one of the disjuncts, the fifth yields the other disjunct. For example:

> Either it is day or it is night.
> It is not night.
> Therefore, it is day.

DIOGENES LAERTIUS

The translations have been made from the text of Cobet, and all deviations therefrom are noted.

Vitae VII, 68 ff.

Of propositions, some are atomic and some are molecular, as the followers of Chrysippus, Archedemus, Athenodorus, Antipater, and Crinis say. Atomic propositions are those consisting of one proposition not repeated.

For example, "It is day." Molecular propositions are those consisting either of one proposition repeated or of more than one proposition. An example of the former is, "If it is day, then it is day,"[33] and of the latter, "If it is day, then it is light."

. . . A negative proposition[34] is one like "It is not day." The double-negative proposition is a kind of negative. For a double negation is the negation of a negation. For example, "Not: it is not day." It asserts, "It is day."

Vitae VII, 71 ff.

Of molecular propositions, the conditional, according to Chrysippus in his *Dialectic* and Diogenes in his *Art of Dialectic* is one formed by the conditional connective "if." This connective announces that the second proposition follows from the first. For example, "If it is day, then it is light." An inferential proposition, according to Crinis in his *Art of Dialectic*, is one which consists of an antecedent proposition and a consequent proposition, joined by the connective "since." For example, "Since it is day, it is light." This connective announces that the second follows from the first and that the first is true. A conjunction is a proposition composed by means of conjunctive connectives. For example, "It is day and it is light." A disjunction is a proposition composed by means of the disjunctive connective "or." For example, "Either it is day or it is night." This connective announces that one or the other of the propositions is false.

Vitae VII, 73.

Among propositions, those are contradictories of one another, with respect to truth and falsehood, of which the one is the negation of the other. For example, "It is day" and "It is not day." Thus a true conditional is one in which the contradictory of the consequent is incompatible with the antecedent. For example, "If it is day, then it is light"—for this is true, since "it is not light," the contradictory of the consequent, is incompatible with "It is day." A false conditional, on the other hand, is one in which the contradictory of the consequent is compatible with the antecedent, as, "If it is day, Dion is walking." For "Dion is not walking" is not incompatible with "It is day."

---

[33] Cobet, p. 174, line 26. After ἐστίν, I should (with Hicks) add ἡμέρα ἐστίν, obtaining

εἰ ἡμέρα ἐστίν, ἡμέρα ἐστίν

which occurs at Sextus, *Adv. Math.* VIII, 110, as the illustration of this same sort of proposition (i.e., a nonsimple repeated proposition, composed of two occurrences of the same proposition).

[34] Cobet, p. 174, line 33. Here again I follow Hicks, with ἀποφατικὸν μέν instead of ἀξιώματος.

Vitae VII, 76 ff.

An argument, according to the followers of Crinis, is composed of a major premise, a minor premise, and a conclusion. For example:

> If it is day, then it is light.
> It is day.
> Therefore, it is light.

For the major premise is "If it is day, then it is light"; the minor premise is "It is day"; and the conclusion is "It is light." A mood is a sort of schema of an argument:

> If the first, then the second.
> The first.
> Therefore, the second.

A schematic argument is a combination of both:

> If Plato lives, then Plato breathes.
> The first.
> Therefore, the second.

The schematic argument is introduced, in long combinations of arguments, in order that we may avoid having to state a long minor premise and the conclusion, and that we may instead say succinctly, "The first. Therefore, the second."

Of arguments, some are conclusive and some are inconclusive. Inconclusive arguments are those which are such that the denial of the conclusion is compatible with the conjunction of the premises:

> If it is day, then it is light.
> It is day.
> Therefore, Dion is walking.

Vitae VII, 79 ff.

Further, of arguments, some are true and others are false. True arguments are those which make correct inferences from true premises. For example:

> If virtue is beneficial, then vice is hurtful.
> Virtue is beneficial.
> Therefore, vice is hurtful.

False arguments are those which either have a false premise or are inconclusive:

> If it is day, then it is light.
> It is day.
> Therefore, Dion is alive.

Arguments may be divided also into possible and impossible, necessary and not necessary. Also, there are certain undemonstrated (because they need no demonstration) arguments, five in number according to Chrysippus (although authorities differ on this), by means of which every argument is constructed. They are assumed in valid arguments, whether syllogistic or schematic (τροπικῶν). A type 1 undemonstrated argument is one in which the whole argument is composed of a conditional and its antecedent, and having the consequent for a conclusion. For example:

> If the first, then the second.
> The first.
> Therefore, the second.

A type 2 undemonstrated argument is one in which, from a conditional and the contradictory of its consequent, the contradictory of its antecedent is concluded. For example:

> If it is day, then it is light.
> But it is night.
> Therefore, it is not day.[35]

Here the minor premise is the contradictory of the consequent, and the conclusion is the contradictory of the antecedent. A type 3 undemonstrated argument is one which, from the denial of a conjunction and from one of the conjuncts, concludes the contradictory of the other conjunct. For example:

> Not both: Plato is dead and Plato is alive.
> Plato is dead.
> Therefore, Plato is not alive.

A type 4 undemonstrated argument is one which, from a disjunction and one of the disjuncts, concludes the contradictory of the other conjunct. For example:

> Either the first or the second.
> The first.
> Therefore, not the second.

A type 5 undemonstrated argument is one in which the whole argument is composed of a disjunction and the contradictory of one of the disjuncts, and which concludes the other disjunct.[36] For example:

> Either it is day or it is night.
> It is not night.
> Therefore, it is day.

---

[35] See chap. v, note 56.
[36] Something seems to be wrong with the text here. See the parallel accounts cited in chap. v, note 54.

Vitae VII, 81.

According to the Stoics, a true proposition follows from a true proposition; for example, "It is light" follows from "It is day." And a false proposition follows from a false proposition; for example, "It is dark" follows from the false proposition "It is night." And also a true follows from a false; for example, "The earth exists" follows from "The earth flies." But a false proposition does not follow from a true one; for example, "The earth flies" does not follow from "The earth exists."

GALEN

The translations of passages in the *Institutio Logica* have been made from the text of Kalbfleisch; that of the passage from *Historia Philosopha* has been made from the text of Diels (*Doxographi Graeci*).

Inst. Log., p. 3, lines 12 ff.

Granting that Theon is identical with Dion and Philo is identical with Dion, it will follow from these that Theon is identical with Philo, because things identical with the same·thing are identical with each other. Thus this demonstration is composed of three parts: first, that which was said first, "Theon is identical with Dion"; second, that which came next, "Philo is identical with Dion"; and third, in addition to these, "Things identical with the same thing are identical with each other." And from these it will be concluded that Theon is identical with Philo. This is the so-called conclusion, and a premise is that from the assumption of which this is concluded . . .

If, having prior knowledge by perception or by demonstration, we assert something about the nature of things, let this assertion be called a "protasis,"[37] which is in accordance with the usage of the ancients, too. And, for any statement that is of itself credible to the intellect, they have used the term "axiom." For example, "Things identical to the same thing are identical." Others call every assertoric statement an "axiom" or a "proposition" . . .[38]

Inst. Log., p. 5, lines 22 ff.

Therefore, for the sake of clarity and concise teaching, we call all such protases "categorical," and the parts from which they are compounded we call "terms," following ancient usage. For example, in "Dion walks"

---

[37] I render πρότασις by "protasis" to avoid using the term "proposition" for both Peripatetic πρότασις and Stoic ἀξίωμα.

[38] Kalbfleisch, p. 4, lines 19 ff. The text is obviously corrupt here.

are the terms "Dion" and "walks," and we take "Dion" for the subject and "walks" for the predicate.

Inst. Log., p. 7, lines 12 ff.

Another kind of protasis consists of those in which we make the assertion not about the existence of the facts but about something being so if something else is so, and something being so if something is not so. Let such protases be named "hypothetical": some, when they say that if something else is so, then this is necessarily so, are *continuous;* and others, when they say either that if something else is not the case, then this is, or that if something else is, then this is not, are *discontinuous.*[39]

Inst. Log., p. 8, lines 5 ff.

. . . these [notions], when they are expressed by sounds, are called "propositions" by the ancient philosophers.

Inst. Log., p. 8, lines 12 ff.

Most frequently people call such protases as "If it is not night, it is day" discontinuous, but they have also been named "disjunctive propositions" by some of the newer philosophers, just as the other form of hypothetical protasis, which we call "continuous," is termed by them "conditional." A more customary way of talking is to apply the term "disjunction" to propositions which we said were called "discontinuous protases," and to apply it in virtue of the connective "or"—and it makes no difference whether "or" is pronounced in one syllable or in two—more customary, that is, than to apply it to conditionals in virtue of the "if" or "if,"[40] if in fact these are synonymous.[41] For example, such a statement as "If it is day, then the sun is over the earth" is called a "conditional proposition" by the newer philosophers; but by the ancients, a "continuous hypothetical protasis." And such a proposition as "Either it is day or it is night" is called a "disjunctive proposition" by the newer philosophers; but a "discontinuous hypothetical protasis" by the ancients. The discontinuous protasis seems to have the same force as such a statement as this: "If it is not day, then it is night," which, when it is said in a conditional form of speech, is called a "conditional" by those who pay attention to the sounds only, but a "disjunction" by those who pay attention

---

[39] 7,12 ff. Orth's translation of this passage seems misleading in its suggestion that the discussion somehow concerns things and their properties.

[40] See note 5.

[41] 8,22. Kalbfleisch, following Prantl, has added ἢ ἐπεί after εἰ, presumably in order to provide some antecedent for αὐτοι. It has been suggested that it would be more reasonable to supply ἢ εἴπερ here, for then there would be an exact parallel with the case of ἢ and ἤτοι just mentioned. This suggestion is plausible, even though it would create the sequence εἰ ἢ εἴπερ εἴπερ.

to the nature of what is meant. Similarly, such a form of speech as "If it is not night, then it is day" is a disjunctive proposition by the nature of what is meant, but in speech it has the form of a conditional.

Such a state of affairs exhibits complete incompatibility, and the other exhibits partial incompatibility, with respect to which we say, "If Dion is at Athens, Dion is not at the Isthmus." For it is generally characteristic of incompatability that the incompatibles cannot both hold, but incompatibility is distinguished into kinds by the fact that some incompatibles (in addition to the impossibility that both hold) cannot both be false, while some, on the contrary, can both be false. Thus, whenever incompatibles have only the one property that they cannot both hold, the incompatibility is partial, but whenever they have also this property—that they cannot both fail to hold—the incompatibility is complete.[42]

Inst. Log., p. 10, lines 13 ff.

If propositions which have neither the relation of logical consequence nor that of incompatibility to one another should be said in other words, we shall call the resulting proposition a "conjunction," as in the case of "Dion walks and Theon converses." These propositions, having neither the relation of consequence nor that of incompatibility, are uttered conjunctively . . . The followers of Chrysippus, fixing their attention more on the manner of speech than on the things spoken about, use the term "conjunction" for all propositions compounded by means of the conjunctive connectives, whether they are consequents of one another or incompatibles.

Inst. Log., p. 11, lines 23 ff.

Now let us distinguish the names of these [moods]. Therefore, in consideration of clarity together with conciseness of teaching, there is no reason not to call propositions containing complete incompatibles "disjunctions," and those containing partial incompatibles "quasi-disjunctions." It makes no difference whether we say "quasi" or "similar." Also, in some propositions, it is possible not only for one part to hold, but several, or even all; but it is necessary for one part to hold. Some call such propositions "pseudo-disjunctions," since disjunctions, whether composed of two atomic propositions or of more, have just one true member. For "Dion walks" is one atomic proposition, and likewise "Dion sits"; and "Dion lies down" is also one proposition, as also are

[42] 9,17–10,2. Here again, Orth's translation fails to reveal the sense. It is essential here to avoid the word *Widerspruch*, which ordinarily means a conjunction of what are here being called "complete incompatibles." Cf. note 39.

"Dion runs" and "Dion stands"; but from all of these arises the disjunction, that is, "Dion either walks, sits, lies down, runs, or stands." Whenever a proposition is put together in this way, any one among the parts is partially incompatible with each of the others, but all collectively are completely incompatible with each, since it is necessary that one of them hold and that the other not hold.[43]

Inst. Log., p. 13, lines 10 ff.

In the continuous hypothetical protasis, which the followers of Chrysippus call a "conditional proposition," if we assume the antecedent as a minor premise we get the consequent as a conclusion, and if we assume the contradictory of the consequent as a minor premise we get the contradictory of the antecedent, but if we assume the consequent or the contradictory of the antecedent we do not get any conclusion.[44]

Inst. Log., p. 15, lines 8 ff.

And the Dialecticians apply the name "mood" to the schemata of arguments. In the argument which, from a conditional and the antecedent, yields the consequent, and which Chrysippus calls a type 1 undemonstrated argument, the mood or schema is as follows:

> If the first, then the second.
> The first.
> Therefore, the second.

In the argument proceeding from a conditional and the contradictory of its consequent to the contradictory of the antecedent, which Chrysippus calls a type 2 undemonstrated argument, the schema is:

> If the first, then the second.
> Not the second.
> Therefore, not the first.

Likewise, in his type 3 argument, which, from the denial of a conjunction and from one of the conjuncts, concludes the contradictory of the other conjunct, the schema is:

> Not both the first and the second.
> The first.
> Therefore, not the second.

---

[43] 12,15–18. Orth's translation is again mistaken. Given a disjunction of n propositions, of which exactly one can be true, it follows that each of the propositions is completely incompatible with the disjunction of the remaining propositions; and that is what I take Galen to be pointing out.

[44] For my translation of προσλαμβάνω, see the Glossary, s.v. πρόσληψις.

Similarly in his type 4 argument, which, from a disjunction and one of the disjuncts, concludes the contradictory of the other disjunct, the schema is as follows:

> Either the first or the second.
> The first.
> Therefore, not the second.

And also in the type 5 argument, which, from a disjunction and the contradictory of one of the disjuncts, concludes the other disjunct, the schema is:

> Either the first or the second.
> Not the first.
> Therefore, the second.

Inst. Log., p. 32, lines 13 ff.

And the Stoics call continuous hypothetical protases "conditional propositions," and discontinuous hypothetical protases "disjunctions"; they agree that there are two syllogisms for the conditional proposition and two for the disjunction. It has been proved elsewhere that not a single syllogism formed from a negated conjunction is of any use in demonstration, just as there is, as they say, no sixth, seventh, eighth, ninth, nor any other syllogism; but now we are concerned only to discuss those that are useful, leaving aside the refutations of those that are superfluously added. The type 3 undemonstrated argument of Chrysippus and his followers is that which, from a negated conjunction and one of the conjuncts, concludes the contradictory of the other conjunct, as in the following example:

> Dion is not both at Athens and at the Isthmus.
> He is at Athens.
> Therefore, he is not at the Isthmus.[45]

The Stoics[46] showed that this argument is useful for many proofs throughout life and even in courts of law. And since, of incompatible states of affairs and incompatible assertions, some have complete incompatibility because they cannot both hold or fail to hold, and some have half-incompatibility because they cannot both hold but can both fail to hold, I have thought it proper for this reason to apply the term "disjunction" to those

---

[45] 33,4. I have followed the reading which, as Kalbfleisch says, is required for the sense.

[46] 33,4. Here I follow Orth, taking καὶ τόνδε ἀναπόδεικτον μὲν instead of καὶ τοῦδε παιδίον μὲν.

having complete incompatibility, and simply the term "an incompatibility,"[47] or, more exactly, "a partial incompatibility," to those having partial incompatibility. In these states of affairs, the syllogism mentioned is useful when it is stated in the same language in which Chrysippus stated it, not, however, put together on the basis of a conjunction but on the basis of incompatibles; in this syllogism are involved many differences with respect to the conjunctive proposition. For there are three kinds of contrast among states of affairs: one, incompatibility, in those which never coexist; another, consequence, in those which always coexist; and the third, in those which sometimes coexist and sometimes do not—all the states of affairs which are neither necessary consequents nor necessary incompatibles from the basis of conjunctive propositions, such as, "Dion is walking and Theon is conversing." And it is obvious that the denial of this will be, "Not both: Dion is walking and Theon is conversing." And the minor premise would be, "Dion is walking," or again, "Theon is conversing"; and the conclusion from the former premise is, "Therefore Theon is not conversing," and from the latter premise, "Therefore, Dion is not walking." . . .

On the one hand, therefore, there will be two syllogisms based on complete consequence, just as there will be two others based on complete incompatibility. Let those based on complete consequence be called "the first" and "the second," and those based on incompatibility "the fourth" and "the fifth," since Chrysippus posited it so. But the third, on the other hand, will verbally be the same as Chrysippus', but with respect to the nature of the premises it will not be the same.

Historia Philosopha, 15.

Since an account of the undemonstrated arguments seems to belong to the logical part of philosophy, it is well also to speak of these. They apply the term "undemonstrated syllogism" to syllogisms which carry through the demonstration through their own agency or do not need any outside information. The first is that which, from a conditional and its antecedent, concludes the consequent. For example:

> If it is day, then it is light.
> It is day.
> Therefore, it is light.

The second is that which, from a conditional and the contradictory of

---

[47] I use the term "(an) incompatibility" here for a molecular proposition whose parts are incompatible with one another.

the consequent, concludes the contradictory of the antecedent. For example:

> If it is day, then it is light.
> It is not light.
> Therefore, it is not day.

And the third is that which, from the contradictory of a conjunction and one of the conjuncts, infers the contradictory of the other conjunct. For example:

> It is not both day and night.
> It is day.
> Therefore, it is not night.

The fourth is that which, from a disjunction and one of the disjuncts, concludes the contradictory of the other disjunct. For example:

> Either it is now day or it is now night.
> It is day.
> Therefore, it is not night.

The fifth is that which, from a disjunction and the contradictory of the one disjunct, infers the other disjunct. For example:

> Either it is day or it is night.
> It is not night.
> Therefore, it is day.

MISCELLANEOUS

Gellius, *Noctes Atticae* II, vii, 21.

Therefore the assertion of those who say "The commands of a father are either honorable or base" is not complete, nor can it be regarded as a true and regular disjunction [ὑγιὲς et νόμιμον διεζευγμένον]. For that disjunction lacks the third member, "or are neither honorable nor base."

Gellius, *Noctes Atticae* V, xi, 8–9.

But our countryman Favorinus, when that syllogism which Bias had employed was mentioned, of which the first πρότασις is ἤτοι καλὴν ἄξεις ἢ αἰσχράν, said that it was not established nor was it a fair disjunction, since it was not necessary that one of the two disjuncts be true, which is necessary in a disjunctive proposition.

Gellius, *Noctes Atticae* XVI, viii, 1 ff.

When I wished to be introduced to the science of logic [*dialectica*] and instructed in it, it was necessary to take in hand and learn what the

Dialecticians call "introductions" [εἰσαγωγαί]. Then because at first I had to learn about propositions [περὶ ἀξιωμάτων], which M. Varro calls *profata* at one time, *proloquia* at another, I sought diligently for the *Commentarius de Proloquiis* of L. Aelius . . .

I therefore of necessity returned to Greek books. From these I obtained the following definition of proposition [ἀξίωμα]: "a complete Lekton assertoric in itself" [λεκτὸν αὐτοτελὲς ἀπόφαντον ὅσον ἐφ' αὐτῷ]. . . .

A proposition [ἀξίωμα] therefore, or a *proloquium*, if you prefer, is of this kind: Hannibal was a Carthaginian. Scipio destroyed Numantia. Milo was convicted of murder. Pleasure is neither good nor evil. And in general any saying which is a full and perfect judgment, so expressed in words that it is necessarily either true or false, is called by the Dialecticians ἀξίωμα [proposition], by M. Varro, as I have said, *proloquium*, by M. Cicero *pronuntiatum*, a word, however, which he declared that he used "only until I can find a better one."

But what the Greeks call συνημμένον ἀξίωμα [conditional proposition], some of our people call *adiunctum*, others *conexum*. The following are such as this: "If Plato walks, then Plato moves"; "If it is day, then the sun is over the earth." Again, what they call συμπεπλεγμένον [conjunction], we call *coniunctum* or *copulatum*. For example, "P. Scipio, son of Paulus, was twice consul and triumphed and was censor and was colleague in the censorship of L. Mummius." However, in every conjunction, if one part is false, the whole is said to be false, even if the others are true. For if to all those true statements which I have made about Scipio I add, "and he overcame Hannibal in Africa," which is false, the totality of the statements made conjunctively will not be true, because of this one false statement which is made with them.

There is also another, which the Greeks call διεζευγμένον [disjunctive proposition] and we call *disiunctum*. This is of such a sort as "Pleasure is either good or bad or neither good or bad." All the disjuncts ought to be incompatible with one another, and their contradictories (which the Greeks call ἀντικείμενα) ought also to be incapable of being simultaneously true. Of all the disjuncts, one ought to be true and the others false. But if none of them is true, or all, or more than one, or if the disjuncts are not incompatible, or if their contradictories are not contrary, then that disjunction is false and is called παραδιεζευγμένον [inclusive disjunction]; for example, this case in which the negations are not contrary: "Either you are running or you are walking or you are standing"; for "not to walk" and "not to stand" and "not to run" are not contrary to one another, since what are called "contraries" may not be simultaneously true; for you may at one and the same time neither walk, stand, nor run.

Cicero, *De Fato*, 15.

On this topic Chrysippus exerts his ingenuity. He pretends that the Chaldeans are deceived as much as other diviners, and that they cannot avail themselves of conditional propositions like the following: "If anyone is born under the Dog Star, he cannot be drowned in the sea." But he would rather have them say, "Not both: x is born under the Dog Star and x will drown in the sea." . . . thus the physician will no longer propose what he is certain of in his art in this fashion, "If x's veins are thus agitated, then x has fever," but rather "Not both: x's veins are thus agitated and x does not have fever"; likewise the geometrician will not say, "Great circles on a sphere divide one another into halves," but rather, "Not both: there are great circles on a sphere and these do not divide one another into halves." What proposition is there which cannot in this way be changed from a conditional [*conexo*] to a negated conjunction!

. . . There are many ways of enunciating a proposition, but there is none more distorted than that which Chrysippus hopes the Chaldeans will adopt in order to please the Stoics.

Cicero, *Topica*, 54.

The Dialecticians use the term "first mode of inference" for the inference in which, when you have assumed the first, that which is implied is inferred. When you negate that which is implied in order to negate that which implies, this is called the "second mode of inference." When, on the other hand, you negate any set of conjuncts and assume one or more of these in order to negate what remains, this is called the "third mode of inference."

Cicero, *Topica*, 56–57.

. . . There remain some further modes of the Dialecticians, which modes are based upon disjunctions:

> Either this or that.
> This.
> Therefore, not that.

Likewise:

> Either this or that.
> Not this.
> Therefore, that.

These inferences are valid because it is impossible for more than one proposition in a disjunction to be true.

Of the inferences which I have written immediately above, the former is called the "fourth mode" and the latter is called the "fifth mode" by the Dialecticians. They add further a negated conjunction, thus:

> Not both this and that.
> This.
> Therefore, not that.

This is the sixth mode. The seventh is:

> Not both this and that.
> Not this.
> Therefore, that. [*sic.*]

From these modes innumerable inferences are generated, which make up almost the whole of dialectic. But only those which I have set forth are necessary for this introduction.

Alexander, *In Top.*, ed. Wallies, p. 8, lines 16 ff.

The arguments which the followers of Antipater called "one-premised syllogisms" are not syllogisms but are deficient. For example:

> It is day.
> Therefore, it is light.

> You are breathing.
> Therefore, you are living.

Alexander, *In Top.*, ed. Wallies, p. 10, lines 5 ff.

Nor would anything be a syllogism which did not preserve the use of a syllogism, for example, the "syllogism" in which the conclusion is the same as one of the premises. Such, according to the Stoics, are those which they call "duplicated" and "unanalyzed inferences." Duplicated syllogisms, according to them, are such as the following:

> If it is day, then it is day.
> It is day.
> Therefore, it is day.

Unanalyzed inferences [ἀδιαφόρως περαίνοντες] are those in which the conclusion is the same as one of the premises, as in this one:

> Either it is day or it is light.
> It is day.
> Therefore, it is day.

Alexander, *In An. Pr.*, ed. Wallies, p. 18.

... Such an argument is practically one-premised:

> It is day.
> Not: not: it is day.
> Therefore, it is light.

For "Not: not: it is day" differs from "It is day" only in manner of speech.

Alexander, *In Top.*, ed. Wallies, p. 175, lines 14 ff.

... by means of the fifth so-called undemonstrated [argument], which is the one which, from a disjunction [διαιρετικοῦ] and the denial of one of the disjuncts, concludes the other disjunct ... and the fourth, which, from a disjunction and one of the disjuncts, infers the contradictory of the other.

Alexander, *In An. Pr.*, ed. Wallies, p. 18, lines 14 ff.

For the utility of the syllogism is not possessed by the following:

> If it is day, then it is light.
> It is day.
> Therefore, it is light.

And this is true generally of the arguments called "unanalyzed inferences" by the newer logicians. Such also are the repeated arguments. For example:

> If it is day, then it is day.
> It is day.
> Therefore, it is day.

Alexander, *In An. Pr.*, ed. Wallies, p. 19, lines 5 ff.

The syllogism saying "Either it is day or it is not day," and then assuming in addition one of the disjuncts, whether the negative, "But it is not day," or the affirmative, "But it is day," draws as conclusion either "It is not day" or "It is day," which seem to be the same as what was assumed beforehand, that is, either the same as "But it is not day" or as "But it is day" ...

Alexander, *In An. Pr.*, ed. Wallies, p. 20, lines 3 ff.

... but in disjunctive syllogisms not composed of contradictories, as in those composed of opposites, the conclusion will be not even verbally the same as either of the premises, since in this case the one is not the denial of the other. For in the following:

> Either it is day or it is night.
> It is not day.
> Therefore, it is night.

"It is night" is not the same as either of the assumptions, neither the major nor the minor . . .

Alexander, *In An. Pr.*, ed. Wallies, p. 21, lines 30 ff.

Such also are the arguments of the Stoics. For example, if somebody should say:

> The first is greater than the second.
> The second is greater than the third.
> Therefore, the first is greater than the third.

this necessarily follows, but not syllogistically, unless someone introduces in addition the premise, "That which is greater than the Greater is greater than that which is less than the Greater."

Alexander, *In An. Pr.*, ed. Wallies, p. 262, lines 30 ff.

. . . the younger philosophers wish to apply the term "syllogism" only to arguments that have a major and a minor premise such that the major is either a conditional, a disjunction, or a conjunction . . .

Alexander, *In An. Pr.*, ed. Wallies, p. 374, lines 25 ff.

> If it is not night, then it is day.
> If nothing exists, then it is not night.
> Therefore, if nothing exists, it is day.

Ioannes Philoponus, *In An. Pr.*, ed. Wallies, p. 36.

In addition to these there are those [syllogisms] called ἀμεθόδως περαίνοντες by the Stoics, as if one should argue:

> The first is greater than the second.
> The second is greater than the third.
> Therefore, the first is greater than the third.

This follows necessarily, but not by means of the premises laid down, unless another premise is added: "That which is greater than x is greater than anything less than x." Again:

> A is equal to B.
> B is equal to C.
> Therefore, A is equal to C.

Here again, the conclusion is drawn with necessity but not from the assumptions. For the premise is left out: "Things equal to the same thing are equal to each other."

Ioannes Philoponus, *In An. Pr.*, ed. Wallies, p. 242, lines 27 ff.

. . . and the Peripatetics, following the common usage, call τὰ πράγματα by the same name, πράγματα, and similarly with τὰ νοήματα and similarly also with αἱ φωναί, and again they call the antecedent [τὸ ἡγούμενον] in hypothetical syllogisms τὸ ἡγούμενον and likewise with the consequent [τὸ ἑπόμενον]. For example, "if it is day" is an antecedent [ἡγούμενον], "the sun is over the earth" is a consequent [ἑπόμενον], for the second is consequent upon the first. The whole, "If it is day, then the sun is over the earth," is a conditional [συνημμένον] because the parts are taken together [συνῆφθαι]. The Peripatetics call "But it is day" the minor premise [μετάληψις] because it is taken a second time. For it was already taken once in the antecedent. They call "Therefore, the sun is over the earth" the conclusion [συμπέρασμα]. So for the Peripatetics. The Stoics proceeding in a more novel way, call τὰ πράγματα, τυγχάνοντα, since we wish to reach [τυχεῖν] τὰ πράγματα and they call νοήματα, ἐκφορικά [expressions] because we give utterance externally to whatever we grasp internally by means of intellect; and they call τὰς φωνάς, λεκτά. The antecedent [ἡγούμενον] is called ἡγούμενον by them (in this alone they agree with the Peripatetics), and the ἑπόμενον is called λῆγον, and the συνημμένον is called τροπικόν, since we turn [τρεπόμεθα] from the antecedent to the consequent; for example, "If it is day, then the sun is over the earth." And the μετάληψις they call πρόσληψις (and this remained in usage), and the συμπέρασμα, ἐπιφορά, since it is superimposed [ἐπιφέρεται] on all the others. These are the names which the Peripatetics and the Stoics have used.

Ioannes Philoponus, *In An. Pr.*, ed. Wallies, p. 244, lines 3 ff.

Concerning hypothetical syllogisms, let us speak as follows. Of the hypotheticals which assert existence or nonexistence, some assert consequence and some assert disjunction. And of those asserting consequence, some by positing the antecedent assert the consequent, and some by denying the consequent deny also the antecedent. For example:

> If what approaches is a man, then it is an animal.
> It is a man.
> Therefore, it is an animal.

This is the first mood of the hypotheticals, which from a consequence [ἀκολουθία], by positing the antecedent, asserts the consequent. Again:

> If what approaches is a man, it is an animal.
> But it is not an animal.
> Therefore, it is not a man.

This is the second hypothetical mood, which, by denying the consequent, denies the antecedent, too.

Ioannes Philoponus, *In An. Pr.*, ed. Wallies, p. 244, lines 26 ff.

Again I say that of the syllogisms which assert existence or nonexistence, some assert consequence and some assert disjunction; and of those asserting consequence, some, by supposing the antecedent, assert the consequent, and some, by denying the consequent, deny also the antecedent. Thus arise these two moods of the hypothetical syllogism, the first and the second . . .

Philoponus, *In An. Pr.*, ed. Wallies, p. 245, lines 20 ff., 32 ff.

. . . we have to make a negative statement, "That which approaches is not both a horse and a man" (for thus we tell the truth), and then, by positing one, to deny the other—"But it is a man. Therefore, it is not a horse." This is the third mood of the hypothetical syllogisms, namely the one which, from a negated conjunction, by positing the one denies the other . . . therefore, from these there arise two other hypothetical moods, the fourth, which from a disjunction, by positing one member, denies the other member or other members, and a fifth, which from a disjunction, by denying the other member or other members, infers the remaining one. An example of the former:

> 5 is even or odd.
> 5 is odd.
> Therefore, 5 is not even.

and of the latter:

> The diagonal is either commensurate with the side or incommensurate.
> It is not commensurate.
> Therefore, it is incommensurate.

Scholia to Ammonius, *In An. Pr.*, ed. Wallies, Praefatio, xi.

There are two kinds of hypothetical syllogism: (1) the simple, and (2) the mixed. The simple is called the "hypothetical with three terms" and the "perfect hypothetical":

> If the sun is over the earth, then it is day.
> If it is day, then it is light.
> Therefore, if the sun is over the earth, then it is light.

There are five kinds of mixed syllogism: the conditional, the pseudo-conditional, the disjunction, the quasi-disjunction, and the pseudo-disjunction. We pass over the syllogism *per impossible*, since it is formed of two hypothetical syllogisms together with one categorical, and not out of one hypothetical and one categorical.

Conditional: There are two kinds of conditional syllogism. Either (1) by positing the antecedent it infers the conclusion,

> If man, then also animal.
> But A.
> Therefore, B.

which is called "first undemonstrated." Or (2) by denying the conclusion it denies the antecedent,

> If man, then also animal.
> If not animal, then not man.

which is called "second undemonstrated" and, by the newer philosophers, "transposition by opposite." Such also is the syllogism which says:

> If not animal, then not man.
> If man, then animal.

For not only does the negative deny the affirmative, but also the affirmative denies the negative.

Pseudo-conditional: A syllogism is pseudo-conditional when the hypothesis and the minor premise, being opposed to one another, lead to a single conclusion. For example:

> If [whether] the soul is mortal or immortal, one must take good care of it.
> But the soul is either mortal or immortal.
> Therefore, one must take good care of it.

> If [whether] the stars are even or odd, they are enumerable.
> The stars are even or odd.
> Therefore, they are enumerable.

> If [whether] there are punishments in Hades or not, one ought to have a care
>   for justice.
> Either there are punishments in Hades or not.
> Therefore, one ought to have a care for justice.

Such, too, is the following argument of Aristotle in the *Protrepticus:*

> Whether one must philosophize or not, one must philosophize.
> Either one must philosophize or not,
> Therefore, one must philosophize.

And such is Plato's argument in the *Protagoras:*

> Whether Protagoras speaks truly or speaks falsely, he speaks falsely.
> But either he speaks truly or he speaks falsely.
> Therefore he speaks falsely.

Such also is the περιτροπή of Tisias and Corax:

> Whether I win or lose, I shall collect.
> I shall win or I shall lose.
> Therefore, I shall collect.
>
> Whether I win or lose, I shall not pay.
> I shall win or I shall lose.
> Therefore, I shall not pay.

Being confounded by these, the judges said, "A bad egg of a bad crow."[48]

Disjunction: The disjunctive syllogism proceeds on the basis of complete incompatibles. They are both constructive and destructive.

> Either it is day or it is night.
> It is day.
> Therefore, it is not night.
>
> Either it is day or it is night.
> It is not day.
> Therefore, it is night.

Quasi-disjunction: This is also called the syllogism "from a negated conjunction." By asserting something in a negated conjunction, it denies something. For example:

> He is not both at Athens and at Megara.
> He is at Athens.
> Therefore, he is not at Megara.

Pseudo-disjunction: It proceeds on the basis of propositions that are not contradictory. For example:

> Either Socrates is walking or Socrates is talking.

---

[48] See Sextus, *Adv. Math.* II, 97 ff., for this story. The teacher's name was "Corax" ("crow").

APPENDIX B

This Glossary is not intended to be a complete list of the technical terms in Stoic logic. It includes only terms that appear in a sufficient number of contexts to establish their technical usage. Further, only a few of the more important occurrences of each term are cited. Usually these will include a definition or at least a passage of relatively clear meaning. Other glossaries of Stoic terminology are as follows:

R. G. Bury, *Sextus Empiricus*, volume 3. This glossary is almost worthless in regard to logical terminology.

I. M. Bocheński, *Elementa Logicae Graecae*, pp. 99 ff. (Greek-Latin). Good.

J. W. Stakelum, *Galen and the Logic of Propositions*, pp. 92–93 (Greek-English). Good.

See also the Index Verborum in volume 4 of *Stoicorum Veterum Fragmenta*. Most of the Aristotelian commentators are well indexed, but unfortunately the indices for Sextus are very incomplete, and there are none for Diogenes Laertius.

It is believed that the abbreviations used in this Glossary will be self-explanatory.

GLOSSARY

ἀδιαφόρως περαίνοντες, s. v. περαίνω.

αἰτιῶδες (ἀξίωμα) Causal proposition, i.e., a molecular proposition compounded by means of the connective "because" (διότι). DL VII 72, 73.

ἀκολουθέω To follow from, as the consequent follows from the antecedent in a true conditional. DL VII 71; SE Math VIII 111. The word was ambiguous, owing to the controversy over the truth-conditions of conditionals. SE Math VIII 112. ⌜q follows from p⌝ was *not* regarded as interchangeable with ⌜if p then q⌝. AlAPr 373,31–35. Interchangeable with ἕπομαι, DL VII 74, 81.

ἀκολουθία Logical consequence. See ἀκολουθέω.

ἀκόλουθον That which follows. DL VII 74. See ἀκολουθέω.

ἀλήθεια 1–4. Truth, corresponding to the first four senses of ἀληθής. 5. Truth, the ruling part of the soul qua in a certain condition. SE Math VII 38 ff.; SE Hyp II 81 ff.

ἀληθής, opp. ψεῦδος 1. True (of propositions). DL VII 66; SE Math VIII 11; SCat 406,22. 2. True (of propositional functions with a time-variable). Bo 234; SVF I 489. In this usage, "It is day" is true at t if and only if "It is day at t" is true in sense 1. 3. True (of arguments); an argument is true if and only if it is valid and has true premises. DL VII 77; SE Math VIII 411; SE Hyp II 138 ff. 4. True (of presentations). SE Math VII 244. Interchangeable with ὑγιής, SE Math VIII 111 ff., 125, 245 ff.

ἀμεθόδως περαίνοντες, s.v. περαίνω.

ἀνάλυσις (συλλογισμῶν) Analysis, the procedure of reducing a given argument (λόγος) or syllogism (συλλογισμός) to a series of the five simple undemonstrated arguments. SE Math VIII 223, 229, 231, 235, 240; Galen (SVF II 248).

ἀναπόδεικτος Undemonstrated (of arguments). The term was applied to the five basic arguments and also, apparently, to all arguments derivable from these. SE Math VIII 223, 228; SE Hyp II 157 ff.; DL VII 79 ff.; Galen Inst 15; DG 607–608. See chap. vi, note 30, and table 2. ἁπλοῦς ά, one of the five basic arguments. οὐχ ἁπλοῦς ά, an argument reducible to the five basic arguments. SE Math VIII 228 ff.

ἀντικείμενον The contradictory (of a proposition); two propositions are contradictory if one is the result of prefixing "not" to the other. SE Math VIII 88 ff.; DL VII 73; Anecdota Graeca 484,20; Ap 266; Bo 261. Cf. ἀποφατικόν.

ἀξίωμα Proposition, a complete λεκτόν assertoric by itself. DL VII 65; Gel XVI 8.1; SE Hyp II 104; SE Math VII 38; VIII 11. Also characterized as "that which is true or false." DL VII 66; SE Math VIII 11; SCat 406,22. ἀ.=πρότασις. AmAPr 26,36.

ἀ.=ἀποφαντικὸς λόγος. AmDI 2,26; Proclus (SVF II 200). τὸ ἀπλοῦν ἀ., atomic proposition. τὸ οὐχ ἀπλοῦν ἀ., molecular proposition. SE Math VIII 93; DL VII 68.

ἀπέραντος, opp. περαντικός Invalid. DL VII 77–78. See περαίνω; cf. ἀσύνακτος. Epictetus Manual 44; SE Hyp II 146 ff., 152–153.

ἀπόδειξις Demonstration, a valid argument which has true premises and reveals a nonevident conclusion. SE Math VIII 305–314; SE Hyp II 140–143; DL VII 45. The relation between ἀπόδειξις and the ἀναπόδεικτοι λόγοι is unclear; see ἀναπόδεικτος.

ἀπόφασις The negative particle "not" (οὐ, οὐχ, οὐχί, οὐκ). SE Math VIII 89, 90; Anecdota Graeca 484,20.

ἀποφατικόν, opp. καταφατικόν Negative proposition, formed by prefixing "not" to a proposition. DL VII 69, 73. The propositions ἡμέρα ἐστίν and οὐχ ἡμέρα ἐστίν are both ἀντικείμενα with respect to one another, but only the latter is ἀποφατικόν. Cf. DL VII 73; SCat 403,32. ὑπεραποφατικόν, a double negation. DL VII 69.

ἄρα Therefore. Used to introduce the conclusion of an argument, never the consequent of a conditional.

ἀρχόμενον The antecedent proposition in a conditional. DL VII 74; SE Math VIII 113–117. Interchangeable with ἡγούμενον, correlative with λῆγον.

αὐτοτελής, s. v. λεκτόν.

δεύτερος, s. v. πρῶτος.

διαλεκτική Logic. According to Chrysippus, it was the science of σημαίνοντα and σημαινόμενα, i.e., of signs and significates. DL VII 43, 62. For other definitions see DL VII 62; SE Math XI 187; AlTop 1,10.

διεζευγμένον An exclusive disjunction, i.e., a molecular proposition compounded by means of the connective (exclusive) "or" (ἤ). DL VII 72; SE Hyp II 191; Galen Inst. 8, 14, 18, et passim. (see Index Verborum); Gel XVI 8.12 (δ. = disiunctum). See also table 2, places cited for arguments 4 and 5.

διφορούμενον (ἀξίωμα) A duplicated proposition, i.e., a molecular proposition compounded of two occurrences of the same proposition: "If it is day, it is day," "It is day or it is day." (On the διφορούμενον–διαφορούμενον question, see Prantl, p. 445, note 122.) SE Math VIII 108 ff. Cf. SE Math VIII 93, 95, 281, 466; DL VII 68; SE Hyp II 112.

διφορούμενος λόγος, a two-premised argument having a δ. for major premise. AlTop 10,7.

ἐλλιπής, s. v. λεκτόν.

ἐπιφορά The conclusion of an argument. DL VII 45, 76, 77; SE Hyp II 135, 136, 174, 175; SE Math VIII 301, 386, 388. Interchangeable with συμπέρασμα. SE Hyp II 136; SE Math VIII 223 ff., 415 ff.

ἔπομαι Synonymous with ἀκολουθέω, q.v.

ἐπόμενον Synonymous with ἀκόλουθον, q.v.

ἡγούμενον The antecedent proposition in a conditional, i.e., the component proposition which immediately follows the connective "if." SE Math VIII 110, 304; DL VII 73, 80; SE Hyp II 111 ff., 148 ff., 189 ff. ἤ. was also the Peripatetic term for "antecedent." PhAPr 242,29–243,6. Cf. Themistius APr 91,32 ff.; AmAPr 68,7. Interchangeable with ἀρχόμενον, q.v.; correlative with λῆγον.

θέμα A meta-principle for the analysis of syllogisms. DL VII 77; Galen (SVF II 248); AlAPr 284,15; 164,31. For the first θέμα, see Ap 277, ed. Oud.; for the third, AlAPr 278,6 ff., and Simplicius, In De Caelo 236,33, ed. Heiberg. See also SE Math VIII 231.

καθηγούμενον A true antecedent in a true conditional. SE Math VIII 244 ff.

καταφατικόν, opp. *ἀποφατικόν*, q.v. Affirmative proposition, i.e., a proposition without the prefix "not."

κατηγόρημα A predicate, i.e., a deficient *λεκτόν* which combines with a subject (*πτῶσις*) to form a proposition. DL VII 58, 64; SE Hyp II 230.

κυριεύω To have scope over —. SE Math VIII 88, 96.

λεκτόν The significate, i.e., that which is signified by a sign (to be distinguished from the object to which the sign refers). SE Math VIII 11 ff. See chap. iii. *λ. αὐτοτελές*, a complete λ., e.g., a proposition, a question, etc. *λ. ἐλλιπές*, a deficient λ., e.g., a subject, a predicate. See chap. iii.

λῆγον The consequent proposition in a conditional, the component proposition which does not immediately follow the connective "if." SE Math VIII 110. Correlative with *ἡγούμενον*, q.v. The equivalent Peripatetic term was *ἑπόμενον*. PhAPr 243,6; AlAPr 177,25 ff.

λῆμμα 1. Premise (of an argument). DL VII 45, 77; SE Hyp II 135 ff., 172 ff.; Galen Inst 4,8; 20,5. 2. Major premise of a two-premised argument. DL VII 76. See *πρόσληψις*.

λόγος This word was used in its ordinary wide sense by the Stoics. In addition, they seem to have used it almost technically in the following two senses: 1. A sentence. Nouns, verbs, connectives, etc., are classed as *μέρη λόγου*. DL VII 57 ff.; Anecdota Graeca 840,2; SE Math I 132 ff. 2. Argument, a system of propositions consisting of premises and a conclusion. DL VII 45, 76; SE Hyp II 135; III 52. Cf. SE Hyp I 202. *λ. ἀληθής*, s. v. *ἀληθής* (3) *λ. ἀποδεικτικός* = *ἀπόδειξις*, q.v. SE Hyp II 140; SE Math VIII 411 ff.

λογότροπος An argument-schema—half argument and half schema. DL VII 77; SE Math VIII 306.

μάχομαι To be incompatible with —. ⌜*p* is incompatible with *q* if and only if it is not possible that both be true.[1] Galen Inst 9,20 ff.; Anecdota Graeca 484,16–17; DL VII 73, 77; SE Hyp II 111; SE Math VIII 119.

μοχθηρός, opp. *ὑγιής*. 1. False (of propositions). SE Hyp II 105, 111; SE Math VIII 248. 2. Invalid (of arguments). SE Hyp II 150, 154. 3. Invalid (of schemata). SE Hyp II 146, 147, 154; SE Math VIII 413, 414, 429, 432, 444.

ὄνομα The name of an individual. DL VII 57; Galen (SVF II 148); Anecdota Graeca 842,19–20.

παραδιεζευγμένον An inclusive disjunction, i.e., a molecular proposition composed of compatible propositions by means of the connective "or" (*ἤ*). Galen Inst. 12,2 ff.; Anecdota Graeca 485,11 ff.; 489,4 ff.; SVF II 217. Cf. Preface to AmAPr, xi–xii; Gel XVI 8.14.

παρασυνημμένον An inferential proposition, i.e., a molecular proposition compounded by means of the connective "since" (*ἐπεί*). DL VII 71, 74.

περαίνω To conclude validly (transitive), to yield as conclusion. Galen Inst (see Index Verborum); DL VII 45 (see SVF II 235); DL VII 195; SE Math VIII 428–429. *ἀδιαφόρως περαίνοντες* Arguments in which the conclusion is the same as one of the premises. AlTop 10,10. Cf. SVF II 248, 259, 261. *ἀμεθόδως περαίνοντες* Arguments which are valid but not syllogistic because they lack an analytic premise. AlAPr 21, 30 ff.; 68,21 ff.; 345,24.

περαντικός Valid. DL VII 78; Galen Inst 49,2; AlAPr 373,34. Interchangeable with *συνακτικός*.

πρᾶγμα τὸ σημαινόμενον πρᾶγμα = *λεκτόν* SE Math VIII 11; DL VII 57.

προσηγορία The name of a class. DL VII 58, Anecdota Graeca 842,19 ff. Cf. Galen Inst 33,12; 11,22; SE Hyp II 227.

πρόσληψις Minor premise of a two-premised argument. DL VII 76; PhAPr 243,8 (cf. Themistius APr 92,17 and AmAPr 68,8); AlAPr 262,28 ff.; SE Math VIII 413.

πρῶτος, δεύτερος, τρίτος, etc. Propositional variables. Ap 279; DL VII 77; SE Math VIII 306. See also the schemata cited in table 2.

πτῶσις Subject, a deficient λεκτόν which combines with a predicate (κατηγόρημα) to form a proposition. DL VII 64.

ῥῆμα Verb, a μέρος λόγου having a κατηγόρημα as λεκτόν. DL VII 58; Galen (SVF II 148).

σημαίνω To express; the relation of a sign to its λεκτόν. See chap. iii. SE Math VIII 11 ff.; DL VII 43, 58, 62.

σημεῖον Signal, the antecedent proposition in a true conditional, etc. SE Math VIII 244 ff. See chap. iii.

συλλογισμός Syllogism, an argument of one of the five undemonstrated types, or an argument which can be analyzed into such arguments. According to Philoponus, the terminology associated with the (two-premised) syllogism was as follows (PhAPr 242,27 ff.; cf. Themistius APr 91,32 ff., and AmAPr 68,7 ff.):

PERIPATETIC	STOIC
ἡγούμενον	ἡγούμενον
ἑπόμενον	λῆγον
συνημμένον	τροπικόν
μετάληψις	πρόσληψις
συμπέρασμα	ἐπιφορά

συλλογιστικός Syllogistic, i.e., either derivable from the five undemonstrated arguments or identical with one of them. DL VII 78; AlAPr 373,34; SE Hyp II 149; Galen Inst 16,9.

συμπεπλεγμένον A conjunction, i.e., a molecular proposition compounded by means of the connective "and" (καί). DL VII 72; SE Math VIII 124–125; Gel XVI 8.9 (= coniunctum); Epictetus Diss II, ix, 8. Interchangeable with συμπλοκή, Galen Inst 10,15 ff. συμπλέξαντες, conjoining. SE Math VIII 416 ff.

συμπέρασμα Conclusion. SE Hyp II 136; SE Math VIII 415; Galen Inst 20,4. Interchangeable with ἐπιφορά, q.v.

συμπλοκή A conjunction. Synonymous with συμπεπλεγμένον. Dexippus Cat 22,18, ed. Busse; DL VII 77. See table 2, references cited for argument 3.

συνάγω To conclude validly. Synonymous with περαίνω, q.v.

συνακτικός Valid. Synonymous with περαντικός. SE Math VIII 415 ff.; SE Hyp II 137 ff.

σύνδεσμος Sentential connective. DL VII 57, 58; SE Math VIII 108 ff. σ. συμπεπλεκτικός, conjunctive connective, i.e., "&." DL VII 71. σ. διεζευκτικός, disjunctive connective, i.e., "or." DL VII 72.

συνημμένον Conditional proposition, i.e., a molecular proposition compounded by means of the connective "if" (εἰ). SE Math VIII 109 ff.; DL VII 71. See chap. v, § 1; also τροπικόν.

σχῆμα Schema (of an argument). DL VII 76; SE Math VIII 227, 216; Galen Inst 15,8–9. Interchangeable with τρόπος.

τρίτος, s.v. πρῶτος.

τροπικόν The molecular major premise of an undemonstrated argument, especially a conditional. SE Hyp II 202; AlAPr 262,28 ff.; 264,8; Galen Inst 16,19 ff.; PhAPr 243,6 (cf. AmAPr 68,6–7; Themistius, AnPr 92,7, ed. Wallies); SE Math VIII 440, 442. ὁ διὰ δύο τροπικῶν, an argument of the form:

$$1 \supset 2$$
$$1 \supset \sim 2$$
$$\overline{}$$
$$\sim 1$$

Origen, *Werke*, ed. Koetschau, vol. 2, pp. 166–167.

τρόπος Schema (of an argument). Synonymous with σχῆμα, q.v.

ὑγιής, opp. μοχθηρός, q.v. 1. True (of propositions). Interchangeable with ἀληθής, q.v. SE Math VIII 125–128, 244 ff. 2. Valid (of arguments). Interchangeable with συνακτικός. SE Hyp II 150 ff. 3. Valid (of schemata). SE Math VIII 413, 414.

φωνή Sound (a linguistic sound capable of expressing a λεκτόν). SE Math VIII 11 ff., 80; DL VII 55. See SVF II 139, 142.

ψεῦδος, opp. ἀληθής, q.v. False; to utter a false proposition; ψεύδεσθαι, to tell a lie through ignorance or malice. SE Math VII 42, 44, 45.

SELECTED BIBLIOGRAPHY

EDITIONS

Alexander of Aphrodisias. *Commentarium in Aristotelis Analyticorum Priorum Librum I.* Ed. Maximilian Wallies; Berlin, Reimer, 1883.

———. *Commentaria in Aristotelis Topicorum Libros Octo.* Ed. Maximilian Wallies; Berlin, Reimer, 1891.

Ammonius. *Commentarius in Aristotelis De Interpretatione.* Ed. Adolf Busse; Berlin, Reimer, 1897.

———. *Commentarium in Aristotelis Analyticorum Priorum Librum I.* Ed. Maximilian Wallies; Berlin, Reimer, 1899.

Apuleius. *De Philosophia Libri.* Ed. Paul Thomas; Leipzig, Teubner, 1908.

Arnim, J. von. *Stoicorum Veterum Fragmenta.* Leipzig, Teubner, 1905–1924. 4 vols.

Bekker, I. *Anecdota Graeca.* Oxford, 1814. 3 vols.

Bocheński, I. M. *Elementa Logicae Graecae.* Rome, Aninima Libraria Cattolica Italiana, 1937.

Boethius. *Commentarii in Librum Aristotelis Περὶ Ἑρμηνείας.* Ed. C. Meiser; Leipzig, Teubner, 1877.

Capella, Martianus. *Opera.* Ed. A. Dick; Leipzig, Teubner, 1925.

Cicero. *De Divinatione; De Fato; Timaeus.* Ed. W. Ax; Leipzig, Teubner, 1938.

———. *De Natura Deorum; Academica.* Trans. H. Rackham, Loeb Classical Library; London, Heinemann, 1933.

———. *Topica* (in *Opera Rhetorica*). Ed. G. Friedrich; Leipzig, Teubner, 1893.

Diels, Hermann. *Doxographi Graeci.* Berlin, Reimer, 1879.

———. *Die Fragmente der Vorsokratiker.* Ed. W. Kranz; 6th ed., Berlin, Weidmann, 1951–1952. 2 vols.

Diogenes Laertius. *Lives of Eminent Philosophers.* Trans. R. D. Hicks, Loeb Classical Library; London, Heinemann, 1925. 2 vols.

———. *Vitae Philosophorum.* Ed. C. G. Cobet; Paris, Firmin-Didot, 1878.

Festa, Nicola. *I Frammenti degli Stoici Antichi.* Bari, Laterza e Figli, 1935.

Galen. *Einführung in die Logik.* Trans. E. Orth; Rome, Scuola Salesiana del Libro, 1938.

———. *Institutio Logica.* Ed. Karl Kalbfleisch; Leipzig, Teubner, 1896.

———. *Medicorum Graecorum Opera.* Ed. C. C. Kühn; Leipzig, 1821–1830.

Gellius, Aulus. *The Attic Nights of Aulus Gellius.* Trans. J. C. Rolfe, Loeb Classical Library; London, Heinemann, 1927.

Origen. *Origenes Werke. Buch. V–VIII Gegen Celsus.* Ed. Paul Koetschau; Leipzig, Hinrichs'sche Buchhandlung, 1899. 2 vols.

Pearson, A. C. *The Fragments of Zeno and Cleanthes.* London, C. J. Clay and Sons, 1891.

Philoponus, Ioannes. *Commentaria in Analytica Priora Aristotelis.* Ed. Maximilian Wallies; Berlin, Reimer, 1905.

———. *Commentaria in Analytica Posteriora Aristotelis.* Ed. Maximilian Wallies; Berlin, Reimer, 1909.

Plutarch. *Moralia.* Ed. G. N. Bernardakis; Leipzig, Teubner, 1888–1896.

Proclus. *In Euclidem Commentarium.* Ed. G. Friedlein; Leipzig, Teubner, 1873.

———. *In Platonis Timaeo.* Ed. E. Diehl; Leipzig, Teubner, 1903.

Schneider, R., and G. Uhlig. *Grammatici Graeci*. Leipzig, Teubner, 1878 (vol. 1, fasc. 1), and 1910 (vol. 5).

Seneca. *Epistulae Morales*. Trans. Richard M. Gummere, Loeb Classical Library; London, Heinemann, 1917. 3 vols.

Sextus Empiricus. *Sextus Empiricus*. Trans. R. G. Bury, Loeb Classical Library; London, Heinemann, 1917, 1933.

──────. *Sextus Empiricus*. Ed. I. Bekker; Berlin, Reimer, 1842.

──────. *Opera*. Ed. H. Mutschmann; Leipzig, Teubner, 1912–1914.

Simplicius. *Commentarius in Aristotelis Categorias*. Ed. Karl Kalbfleisch; Berlin, Reimer, 1907.

WORKS

Barth, Paul. *Die Stoa*. Ed. H. Goedeckemeyer; 6th ed., Stuttgart, Frommann, 1946.

Beth, E. W. *Geschiednis der Logica*. 2d ed., The Hague, Servire, 1948.

Bevan, Edwyn. *Stoics and Sceptics*. Oxford, 1913.

Bocheński, I. M. *Ancient Formal Logic*. Amsterdam, North-Holland Publishing Co., 1951.

──────. "De Consequentiis Scholasticorum Earumque Origine," *Angelicum* (Rome), vol. 15 (1938), pp. 1–18.

Brehier, E. *La Théorie des incorporels dans l'ancien Stoïcisme*. Paris, Vrin, 1928.

Brochard, Victor. "Sur la logique des Stoïciens," *Archiv für Geschichte der Philosophie*, vol. 5 (1892), pp. 449–468.

Carnap, Rudolf. *Meaning and Necessity*. University of Chicago Press, 1947.

Chisholm, Roderick. "Sextus Empiricus and Modern Empiricism," *Philosophy of Science*, vol. 8, no. 3 (1941), pp. 371–384.

De Lacy, Phillip. "Stoic Categories as Methodological Principles," American Philological Association, *Transactions*, vol. 76 (1945), pp. 246–263.

De Lacy, Phillip, and Estelle A. De Lacy. *Philodemus: On Methods of Inference*. Lancaster, Pa., Lancaster Press, 1941.

Elorduy, E. *See* Stoic bibliography in *Philologus*. Supplementband 28.3. Leipzig, 1936.

Frege, G. "Ueber Sinn und Bedeutung," *Zeitschrift für Philosophie*, vol. 100 (1892), pp. 25–50.

Gentzen, G. "Untersuchungen über das logische Schliessen," *Mathematische Zeitschrift*, vol. 39 (1935), pp. 176–210, 405–431.

Heintz, Werner. *Studien zu Sextus Empiricus*. Ed. Richard Harder; Halle, Max Niemeyer, 1932.

Hurst, Martha. "Implication in the Fourth Century B.C.," *Mind*, n.s., vol. 44 (1935), pp. 484–495.

Jaskowski, Stanislaw. "On the Rules of Suppositions in Formal Logic," *Studia Logica* no. 1 (Warsaw), 1934.

Kalbfleisch, Karl. "Ueber Galens Einleitung in die Logik," *Jahrbücher für classische Philologie*. Supplementband 23, pp. 681–708. Leipzig, Teubner, 1897.

Kochalsky, Arthur. *De Sexti Empirici Adversus Logicos Libris Questiones Criticae*. Marburg, 1911 (dissertation)

Krokiewicz, Adam. "O Logice Stoików" (On the Logic of the Stoics), *Kwartalnik Filozoficzny*, vol. 17 (1948).

Łukasiewicz, Jan. *Aristotle's Syllogistic*. Oxford, Clarendon Press, 1951.

──────. "Philosophische Bemerkungen zu mehrwertigen Systemen des Aussagenkalkuls," *Comptes Rendus des Séances de la Société des Sciences et des Lettres de Varsovie*, vol. 23 (1930), Classe III, pp. 51–77.

———. "Zur Geschichte der Aussagenlogik," *Erkenntnis*, vol. 5 (1935), pp. 111–131.

Mates, Benson. "Diodorean Implication," *The Philosophical Review*, vol. 58 (1949), pp. 234–242.

———. "Stoic Logic and the Text of Sextus Empiricus," *American Journal of Philology*, vol. 70 (1949), pp. 290–298.

Peirce, C. S. *Collected Papers*. Cambridge, Harvard University Press, 1931–1934. 4 vols.

Pohlenz, Max. *Die Stoa*. Göttingen, Vandenhoeck und Ruprecht, 1948. 2 vols.

Prantl, Carl. *Geschichte der Logik im Abendlande*. Leipzig, Hirzel, 1855.

Quine, W. V. *A Short Course in Logic*. Harvard Co-op Society, 1947 (mimeographed).

Reymond [-Virieux], Antoinette. *La Logique et l'épistémologie des Stoïciens*. Chambéry, Editions "Lire," n.d.

———. "Points de contact entre la logique stoïcienne et la logique russellienne," *International Congress for the Unity of Science*. Paris, 1936.

Rüstow, Alexander. *Der Lügner*. Leipzig, Teubner, 1910 (dissertation).

Schmekel, A. *Forschungen zur Philosophie des Hellenismus*. Berlin, Weidmannsche Verlagsbuchhandlung, 1938.

Scholz, Heinrich. *Geschichte der Logik*. Berlin, Junker und Dünnhaupt, 1931.

———. Review of Orth's translation of Galen, *Institutio Logica*, in *Deutsche Literaturzeitung*, 1939, p. 188.

———. Review of J. W. Stakelum, *Galen and the Logic of Propositions*, in *ibid.*, nos. 37–38 (1941), cols. 866–869.

Stakelum, J. W. *Galen and the Logic of Propositions*, Logicalia no. 2. Rome, Angelicum, 1940.

———. "Why Galenian Figure?" *The New Scholasticism*, vol. 16 (1942), pp. 289–296.

Steinthal, H. *Geschichte der Sprachwissenschaft*. 2d ed., Berlin, F. Dummler, 1890.

Stock, St. George. *Stoicism*. London, Constable, 1908.

Ueberweg, Friedrich. *Grundriss der Geschichte der Philosophie* (Part 1, *Die Philosophie des Altertums*. Ed. K. Praechter). 12th ed., Berlin, E. S. Mittler und Sohn, 1926.

Zeller, Eduard. *Die Philosophie der Griechen*. Ed. Wellman; 5th ed., Leipzig, O. R. Reisland, 1923.

———. *Stoics, Epicureans, and Sceptics*. Trans. O. J. Reichel; London, Longmans, Green and Co., 1880.

———. "Ueber den κυριεύων des Megarikers Diodorus," *Sitzungsberichte der Königlichen Preussischen Akademie der Wissenschaften*. Pp. 151–159. Berlin, 1882.

INDEX TO PASSAGES CITED OR TRANSLATED

References to translations are in italic type.

GENERAL INDEX